a funny time to be gay

ed karvoski jr.

a fireside book
published by simon & schuster

FIRESIDE
Rockefeller Center
1230 Avenue of the Americas
New York, NY 10020

FIRESIDE and colophon are registered trademarks
of Simon & Schuster Inc.

Designed by Brian Mulligan

Manufactured in the United States of America

1   3   5   7   9   10   8   6   4   2

Library of Congress Cataloging-in-Publication Data
A funny time to be gay / [compiled by] Ed Karvoski Jr.
p.   cm.
Collection of monologues with brief introductory remarks.
1. Homosexuality—Humor.   2. Gay men—Humor.
3. Lesbians—Humor.   4. Gay wit and humor.   I. Karvoski, Ed.
PN6231.H57F86   1996
792.7'028'092273—dc20   96-31205
CIP

ISBN 0-684-81896-5

dedicated to

my parents

and jay

contents

introduction

comedy comes out of the closet

Funny how the entertainment industry expects performers who are gay or lesbian to stay in the closet, isn't it? Well, some of today's wittiest wisecrackers are *not* amused. They're "the out generation" of gay and lesbian comics, and their time has come—*fashionably* late, of course!

Thus began a magazine article I wrote in the spring of 1993. As a comedy writer, entertainment journalist, performer, and gay man, I found the subject of gay comics immediately fascinating. And I approached the assignment with added excitement for another personal reason: I'd been writing for gay magazines for several years, but this article was the first for which I didn't use a nom de plume (French for "writer in the closet").

Who could have predicted that only days after I'd received the assignment, the topic would become quite timely? In March of that year, Lea DeLaria broke mainstream ground with a headline-grabbing appearance on *The Arsenio Hall Show.* Ready or not, viewers from coast to coast heard her blare: "It's the 1990s, it's hip to be queer, and I'm a b-i-i-i-g dyke!"

A couple of days after DeLaria's late-night debut, I began researching my article. First stop: Gay & Lesbian Comedy Night at the Comedy Store, located on the Sunset Strip in Los Angeles. The popular humor haven had launched the weekly showcase in January of the same year—on the same day as President Clinton's inauguration. Barry Steiger, who hosted the showcase for its first fourteen months, described the concurrence of the two events as "symbolic—a turning point for America and certainly a turning point for a mainstream comedy club."

By late spring, the attendance at the Gay & Lesbian Comedy Night had grown to capacity, thanks to good word of mouth (giving credence to a saying within the community regarding the quickest means of communication: "telephone . . . telegraph . . . tell a *queen*"). The lineup included a mix of newcomers and seasoned pros, a diverse group with one common message—it's now *in* to be an *out* comic!

Onstage, veteran comic-actor Michael Greer—best known for his starring roles in *Fortune and Men's Eyes* (MGM, 1971) and *The Gay Deceivers* (American International, 1969)—mused, "How can I be *in* and *out* at the same time? It's too exhausting!"

After the show, I was privileged to interview Robin Tyler, the world's first homo humorist since Oscar Wilde. A comic, producer, and political activist, Tyler started performing as an out lesbian in the seventies. Holding court at the Comedy Store that night, she enthusiastically supported the comics who are following in her footsteps. "I love them!" she gushed. "They're like my children!"

Between the emergence of a few trailblazers in the seventies and the surge of fresh funny faces in the gay nineties, a number of entertainers had diligently honed the queer comedy niche. Before mainstream ground was broken, the imminent rumblings of a united effort were felt in the early eighties in San Francisco. The epicenter: the Valencia Rose. "We learned our craft there because we were denied that at other places," recalls Tom Ammiano, dubbed "the Mother of Gay Comedy" by the San Francisco press. Even in so-called gay-friendly San Francisco, he says, straight crowds at mainstream comedy clubs were unreceptive, even hostile, to acts that included lines such as "Homophobia is the fear that three fags will break into your house and redecorate."

Meanwhile, on the East Coast in the eighties, openly gay and lesbian comics began popping up at cabarets, performance spaces, and women's music festivals and coffeehouses. And though the Valencia Rose closed in 1985, a similar venue, Josie's Cabaret & Juice Joint, opened in San Francisco in 1990 and continues to showcase an ever-growing number of out comics.

But why is it, at this particular time, that we're suddenly seeing a proliferation of openly gay and lesbian comics? "Comedy follows the civil rights movements," explains Tyler. "When the focus was on blacks in the 1960s, a lot of black comics came up. When the focus was on feminism in the 1970s, a lot more women comics came up. Now, the focus is on us; we're the civil rights movement that everybody's talking about, so it's only natural that more and more gay and lesbian comics are coming up."

The year 1993 turned full circle for me. In the fall and winter I wrote several more magazine articles about gay and lesbian comics—specifically, about *Out There,* the first gay and lesbian comedy special, which debuted that December on Comedy Central, the all-comedy cable channel. With Lea DeLaria as host, the one-hour special—produced by Trevor Hopkins and Juliet Blake of the English Channel—was taped before a live audience at the historic Great American Music Hall in San Francisco. Appropriately, the show was staged on October 11, National Coming Out Day, an annual event that supports gay men and lesbians who wish to take the next step in their coming-out process. Indeed, the airing of *Out There* to a national television audience was a long overdue step in the right direction for the entertainment industry.

But was Middle America ready to accept gays and lesbians on television—this time *telling* the jokes rather than being the butt of them? "Middle America is having a hard time accepting *short division!*" roared DeLaria when I interviewed her prior to the taping. "I think that if we had waited for Middle America to be ready for civil rights and for feminism, we'd still be waiting," she continued. "I think that in some ways, that argument is homophobic, and it's time to get past that."

The fact is a good number of television viewers were game for the gay and lesbian laugh fest—and, as we all know, numbers is the name of the game in the television industry. According to

Comedy Central, *Out There* attracted double the usual number of viewers for that time slot.

The team of Hopkins and Blake assembled another outstanding lineup for *Out There II,* with Amanda Bearse stepping out of her role as Marcy D'Arcy on *Married . . . with Children* to host the show. Taped at Caroline's Comedy Club in midtown Manhattan, the show had an unusually enthusiastic audience. Then again, it was an unusual week in New York City. *Out There II* was taped in June 1994, smack in the middle of the Stonewall 25 festivities celebrating the birth of the gay rights movement.

As Bearse prepared for the special, she told me that she hoped viewers would glean a message between the laughs: "I hope the message the show relays is that living out of the closet can be a wonderful, rich experience; that it doesn't have to be a scary place to stand in the light."

The actress also shared the fact that she'd love to develop her own sitcom and play a lesbian who would provide a positive image to young TV viewers. If such images had been available when she was growing up, Bearse noted, "It probably would have given me confidence and reassurance that I searched for in my adolescence. It's important to have positive role models."

I'm pleased to have had the opportunity to meet and write about many of the comics who are coming out and, indeed, acting as role models. While writing this book, I had the opportunity to tag along with Bob Smith on the night he became the first openly gay comic to appear on *The Tonight Show.* I had the chance to attend the taping of an episode of *Grace Under Fire* in which Barry Steiger played Grace's proud-to-be-gay in-law. I caught Steve Moore's performance the first night he experimented with a new set of jokes about a delicate subject—his positive HIV status.

I took a close-up look at a piece of history in the making, both for the entertainment industry and for the gay and lesbian community. Through their own words, both onstage and off, I invite you to get to know these talented men and women whom I've enjoyed meeting over the last couple of years.

These performers are debunking the widely held notion among straight audiences that they never come face-to-face with a gay person. For the entertainment industry, they're supplying a voice that has been underrepresented for too long. And for the gay and lesbian community, they're lifting our spirits while we all continue the fight for human rights. From gay cabarets to the television screen, these comics reflect the diversity of the gay and lesbian community as they carry their message: "We're here, we're queer, get used to laughing along with us!" Certainly that diversity is reflected in the range of comics represented in this book.

And before anyone rushes off a letter to the editor of a gay and lesbian publication, I must state that I'm already well aware that not every single openly gay or lesbian comic is profiled within these pages. Space limitations simply did not allow me to include everyone I've met, and time considerations did not allow me to meet with every comic on my wish list. (In an effort to be as comprehensive as possible, I'm including a Comics Listing in this book, with contact information for bookings and public relations.)

An odd memory kept resurfacing as I was writing this book. Several years ago I had a writing gig for a tabloid-style TV program, and while researching a particular story, I needed to riffle through mounds of old, circa-1960s fan magazines. An item about Rock Hudson caught my attention. In an insinuating tone, the report revealed that Rock Hudson was known to *sew his own curtains!* I guess that was the 1960s version of outing!

I thought of that tidbit often as I chatted with openly gay and lesbian comics. These out-and-proud entertainers will never have to live in fear that some gossipmonger will go snooping around their drapery! As Lynda Montgomery says, "My biggest fear is that the *National Enquirer* will say I'm straight!"

To the next generation of showbiz hopefuls who are gay or lesbian and choose not to hide it: make a grand entrance onto the comedy-club stages and television and film studios. The closet door has been set ajar.

As any of these openly gay and lesbian comics will tell you, "A funny thing happened on the way out of the closet . . . !"

—Ed Karvoski Jr.

blazing
trails
in the
seventies

At Los Angeles' famed Comedy Store in 1977, Robin Tyler was being heckled by a bunch of men, one of whom yelled: "Are you a lesbian?" The openly gay comic's retort was spot on: "Are *you* the alternative?" The comedians who followed her (all straight) opened their acts by declaring they were gay, too. "It's funny," says Tyler, "now it's in to be out. I even have straight comics calling me and asking if it's OK to claim to be gay, as a career move!" . . . Being the first to leap out of the closet and onto the comedy circuit hasn't done Canadian-born Tyler's career any harm.

—Jane Nicholls and Karen G. Jackovich,
Who Weekly (Australia), February 1994

robin
tyler

"All of a sudden I'm chic—I'm a lesbian comic!" exclaims Robin Tyler. "I went from even gays and lesbians being scared of me—saying, 'How could you go onstage and be so open?'—to a movement where there's a significant number of comics who are telling the truth."

Tyler captured headlines right from the start of her performing career, in the sixties, as a Judy Garland impersonator at a New York drag bar. Following a police raid—at the time, a routine occurrence at such establishments—she had the dubious honor of being singled out in a *New York Post* headline: 44 MEN AND 1 WOMAN ARRESTED FOR FEMALE IMPERSONATION.

Under contract with ABC in the seventies, Tyler appeared on television comedies with then partner Pat Harrison. Concurrently, she was in the public eye slinging barbs at Anita Bryant in response to antihomosexual attacks: "Anita Bryant is to Christianity what paint-by-numbers is to art." Again, Tyler grabbed headlines—this time as a vociferous activist for the gay and lesbian movement. Hollywood insiders warned the comic that she was jeopardizing her showbiz career, but, Tyler says, "It would have been ridiculous to go onstage and not say, 'I'm a lesbian.' It would have been like Richard Pryor going onstage and saying he was white."

Thus came Tyler's 1978 comedy album, *Always a Bridesmaid, Never a Groom,* her third album but her first as an openly lesbian comic. And in 1979 Tyler became the first openly lesbian or gay comic to appear on national television when she was guest on a Showtime special hosted by Phyllis Diller.

"You cannot be a truly great artist unless you can be honest," Tyler states with the authoritative tone of a schoolteacher. (In fact, she does teach a college course, on the history of comedy.) "There's a therapy saying: 'You're only as sick as your secrets.' Yet gay men and lesbians have been told that we should keep secrets in order to be well. We, as a community, are beginning to not be dysfunctional—we're no longer keeping secrets. And the comedy of gay and lesbian comics is a reflection of what's happening in our community—the pride, and the truth, and the guts to come out."

Now primarily a producer, Tyler has helped launch the careers of numerous lesbian performers via her women's music and comedy festivals. Additionally, she produced the main stage at the 1993 March on Washington (in support of what she calls "gay/lesbian/transsexual/transgender/transvestite—and anything else you can fit on a T-shirt—rights"), as well as the 1994 International Gay & Lesbian Comedy Festival in Sydney,

Australia. "Australia is far more advanced in the area of civil
rights for gays and lesbians than the United States," she observes.
Meanwhile, in a glowing review for the comedy festival, *The
Sydney Morning Herald* affectionately observed: "[Tyler] seems to
be settling into an elder-stateswoman/mother-hen role for the
next wave" of openly gay and lesbian comics.

Indeed, Tyler is proud of her protégés' accomplishments and
their impact. But, she clarifies, "Whether or not we ever have
our own TV sitcom and it works to Iowa, I don't care. What I
care about is that lesbians and gay men are making a change in
the world—especially for each other."

onstage

still a bridesmaid, never a groom

I was walking down the street and a man pointed at me
and started screaming, "I know what you are—you're one
of them *queers!* I think they should take all of you queers
and put you on an island!" And I calmly replied, "Oh, but
they did, darling. They call it Manhattan."

✳   ✳   ✳

When I came out, another dyke asked me, "Are you a
butch or a femme?"

I asked, "What's the difference?"

She said, "Well, the femme does the cooking, the cleaning, the housework, and takes care of the butch's emotional needs."

"And what does the butch do?" I asked.

She said, "The butch makes all the decisions."

"Then I'm a butch," I replied. "And so is my Jewish mother!"

In the seventies, I was told that a lesbian had to be a vegetarian. But I did *not* give up men so I could eat *tofu!*

Being gay or lesbian is not a "lifestyle." Disco was a lifestyle. Being gay or lesbian is about our lives . . . about affectional preference . . . about our right to love. If I never had sex with another woman again, I would still be a lesbian. I wouldn't be a very *happy* lesbian, but I would still be a lesbian.

If homosexuality is a disease, let's all call in queer to work. "Hello, can't work today. Still queer."

* * *

Jerry Falwell is so homophobic he thinks that global warming was caused by the AIDS quilt.

I don't mind born-agains being born again, but why do they have to come back as themselves?!

The pope runs all over the world condemning homosexuality, dressed in high drag. Now I ask you!

Jesus *had* to be a Jewish boy:
    He lived with his family until he was thirty . . .
    He took up his father's profession . . .
    And his mother thought he was God!

* * *

Ban gays and lesbians in the military? Are you kidding? If you took all the lesbians out of the WACS, you'd be left with four typists!

Remember the TV coverage of the Gulf War? CNN kept showing the one straight woman over there. Every hour on the hour, they'd haul her out and they'd say, "This is Captain Mary Smith and she wants to say hi to her husband, Mark, and her son, Johnny." Meanwhile, there's two thousand dykes standing behind her saying, "Hey, Marge, keep my bowling ball polished, OK?"

These dykes in the gulf had no idea there was a war; they thought they were in Palm Springs at the Dinah Shore Golf Tournament!

I hear that Hillary Clinton had an affair in college with one of us. But don't worry—she didn't inhale!

The Republican Party should change their national emblem from an elephant to a prophylactic, because it . . .

1. stands for inflation . . .
2. halts production . . .
3. protects a bunch of pricks, and . . .
4. gives a false sense of security when one is being screwed

san francisco-based comics blossom at the valencia rose in the eighties

The routines of [these] unabashed comics are as offbeat and off-the-wall as anything in San Francisco's burgeoning comedy circuit. But they've been drawing larger legions of delighted fans into what has become the gay community's newest entertainment trend—stand-up comedy. The city's serious gay ideologues may have been getting a lot of P.R. lately, but gay cognoscenti have caught on to the Valencia Rose Cabaret, which is generally believed to be the nation's first gay comedy club. The comedy to be found at the Valencia Rose is as good as— and often better than—anything in the city's mainstream comedy clubs. . . .

Like most entertainment phenomena, the gay comedy vogue comes because of the fortuitous combination of a right place, right time, and the right audiences ready for the right product. Ironically, the epicenter of gay comedy is a funeral home that was converted into the Valencia Rose Cabaret two years ago. With gays eager to find non-sexual social alternatives in the face of the AIDS epidemic, audiences have grown substantially in recent months. About 300 customers now crowd to the three venues or shows at the Valencia Rose on a typical weekend night.

—Randy M. Shilts, "Datebook,"
The San Francisco Chronicle, March 1984

tom
ammiano

"I've thrown my hat and matching shoes into the ring," declared Tom Ammiano, announcing his candidacy for the San Francisco School Board in 1980. Though he lost his first political bid, Ammiano quickly won praise as the city's leading openly gay comic. In 1982, he approached Ron Lanza and Hank Wilson, friends of his who created a community entertainment center. "I suggested to Ron and Hank that we do gay comedy there," Ammiano recalls. "They said, 'What's gay comedy?' I said, 'I don't know. All I know is, I go to straight comedy clubs and I try to be funny, and I talk about being gay, and they want to eat my liver! I need a place to develop.' "

The Valencia Rose became that place for Ammiano and other openly gay and lesbian comics to develop. Mondays became Gay Open Mike Night, an outlet for new talent to experiment. Soon the Saturday time slot was added, known as Gay Comedy Night, which provided a paid gig for the more polished performers. "Soon after the Rose opened, Donald Montwill came in, and he started to do the booking and the managing," Ammiano relates. "But in the beginning there was really nobody to book, because nobody could figure out what the hell gay comedy was!"

It didn't take long for the Valencia Rose to attract a talent pool, though. "It was something people were hungry for," says Ammiano. "At the time, a gay and lesbian culture was starting to develop. Some people painted, some did photography, others made films; we did comedy. We felt good that we started something."

But even before he inaugurated the openly gay comedy showcase, Ammiano, a self-described "pioneer woman," had been breaking ground. As a teacher in San Francisco in the early 1970s, he helped eliminate culturally biased IQ tests. He created the Gay/Lesbian Speakers Bureau to present a gay perspective to high school students and was subjected to a *National Enquirer* tirade: PERVERT TEACHES STUDENTS GAY POSITIONS!

He was instrumental, furthermore, in making condoms available in the middle and high schools, as well as in prohibiting the Boy Scouts from recruiting in the schools because of the Scouts' no-gays policy. "A board member once told me there was no such thing as a gay Boy Scout," says Ammiano. "I said, 'I beg your pardon, I was a gay Boy Scout. I was the Avon representative for my troop!'"

In 1990, Ammiano once again entered the race for the city's school board. "I'm not going to insist that all textbooks be published by the Mapplethorpe Company," pledged the openly gay candidate, "but it *would* be interesting: 'Look, look, Jane. Dick!' " He was elected.

And in 1994, Ammiano won his bid for the San Francisco Board of Supervisors. "I always get humor in there and lighten things up," he says, "but I never trivialize political issues." Supervisor by day, Ammiano still performs as a stand-up comic, making frequent appearances at Josie's Cabaret & Juice Joint, which he describes as "Son of the Rose, a jewel of a place!"

His advice for the next generation of openly gay and lesbian comics? "I hope that they don't assimilate so much that they become indistinguishable. Acceptance is good, but that doesn't mean you have to lose your edge, or your difference."

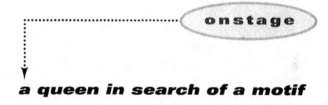

a queen in search of a motif

San Francisco is so gay we even have our own patron saint: Saint Francis the Sissy. For his miracle, he changed breakfast into brunch.

We had a famous mayor in San Francisco—Dianne Feinstein, easily recognizable by her *Planet of the Apes* hairdo.

Dianne is one of those politicians who believes in the two-*perm* limit.

I've been asked if Dianne Feinstein is homophobic. I

don't know, but one time she was on an elevator with the lesbian police commissioner, and when the doors opened someone said, "Going down?" And Dianne said, "*No, no, no. We're just talking!*"

We're lucky in San Francisco, we have Gay Pride Month. A whole *month!* Some places, like Salt Lake City, have the Gay Pride *Minute:* two people with bags over their heads running past the Mormon Tabernacle Temple. "Hi, I'm Donny! I'm Marie!"

*　*　*

I love the month of June. First of all, because it's the name of Beaver's mother. But more than that, it's the time for the annual Gay Pride Parade. That's what we *used* to call it. Nowadays, in San Francisco, they call the event the Gay, Lesbian, Bisexual and Transgender Freedom Day Committee. By the time you say it, the parade is over!

I love the contingents in the parade:

Gay Men, Clean & Sober—otherwise known as *Queen &* Sober.
Gay Cowboys—or, Fags on Nags.
Gay Gurus—they sleep on a bed of nails (Lee Press-On).
Gay Men for Self-Defense—or, Nelly Ninjas.

Lesbian Fathers—they march waving turkey basters over their heads.

Gay Police—they don't read you the Miranda rights; they read you the *Carmen Miranda* rights.

* * *

I moved to San Francisco in 1962; I was so young and innocent. At the time, I *thought* I was in the closet. I wore tight pants, had my hair a little teased, with a little spit curl instead of a sideburn. I sashayed down Castro Street and people yelled, "Faggot!" I wondered, "How did they know? Was it my SAT scores?"

In those days, I was so naive about sex. When I'd carry on with a guy, when he touched my balls, I'd turn my head and cough.

But that was a long time ago. Now I'm fifty years old. Of course, that's *ninety-nine* years old in fag years!

* * *

I travel a lot. And when I travel, I like to fly my favorite airline—Gay Air.

I love the seating on Gay Air—screaming or nonscreaming. On Gay Air, when you assume the crash position, you put your head between someone *else's* knees.

I recently traveled to Texas, where the women are women and the men are Wynonna Judd.

I thought they wouldn't like me in Texas because I'm a fag. However, they were very nice. They gave me a parade in front of the Dallas Book Depository. I was wearing a pink pillbox hat and dress, so I knew I'd be safe.

Then they invited me to a lynchin'—I mean, a *luncheon*.

They're very much into ethnicity in Texas. They said, "Are you Eye-talian?" I said, "No, I-sissy." They said, "You better watch your mouth, boy. How would you like to be hung?" I said, "Give me an option. Please, who wouldn't?!"

Then I went to New Orleans, where they're really into food, and they offered me crawfish. I said, "How do you eat them?" They said, "Suck the head and pull the tail." I said, "That's why I left San Francisco. Give me a break."

Then I headed for New York City, where they gave me a gig befitting my status as an openly gay comic. I opened in the Comedy Corner of the Port Authority men's room.

Then I went to Toronto, which is an Indian name for "many, many, many white people." Homophobic? When they saw that I was from San Francisco they asked me for a blood sample. I failed. All my chromosomes were in the shape of croissants.

suzy berger

Growing up, Suzy Berger would cringe when she was called a *thespian*. "The word 'thespian' is strangely close to the word 'lesbian,' " she says, recalling her long-gone paranoia. Today, both parts of her life—as thespian and lesbian—are strangely integrated.

At age sixteen, Berger attended the American Academy of Dramatic Arts in New York City and earned a bachelor's degree in theater. Auditioning for the program, she remembers, "I did a monologue with an English accent and I was so proud of myself." Then she was told to repeat the performance, sans the foreign dialect. "That was my first lesson: be yourself. That's kind of cool, because I've since learned that that's what stand-up comedy is all about."

Of course, many comics who are gay choose not to share that part of themselves. "That didn't seem to be an option," says Berger, who has performed as an out lesbian since the Valencia

Rose opened in 1982. "Stand-up comedy, to me, is so self-revelatory."

She hopes that her audiences, too, experience some revelations. If she senses discomfort from a straight audience, she says, "I work a little harder. By that I mean I try to be a little freer—not let their judgment get to me, but at the same time acknowledge it. I'll say, 'Do you think it's strange that I'm a lesbian? Does anyone know any lesbians?' I'll work with them to combat that homophobia."

Sound a bit like therapy? Berger thinks so, too: "In psychoanalysis, a person sits on a couch and does a stream of consciousness. What I do isn't unlike that, except that I'm talking to a group of people. And I'm getting constant approval with laughter. What could be more therapeutic than that?"

While still working as a comic and an actress, Berger returned to school and earned a graduate degree in psychology. "I called home and told my mother that I'm studying drama therapy," she recalls, "and she calls off to my dad, 'I don't know, I think she's doing some play at the college.' "

As a lesbian comic, Berger acknowledges—and embraces—her reputation as a rebel. Likewise, as a therapist, she could be described as an iconoclast. "I've worked with clients that other people would choose not to work with," she says. For example, she enthusiastically welcomed a client who was diagnosed with multiple personalities. "I think it's fabulous! I know so many people that don't even have one!"

When she was assigned to work with schizophrenics and manic depressives at a psychiatric hospital, she says, "I was afraid I was going to work with some of my old girlfriends. Then

I thought, look at the bright side—I might meet somebody new!"

With the security of a psychology degree ("because you just don't know"), Berger is amused by a curious irony: currently, her full-time job is working as a funny lesbian thespian! As a stand-up comic, Berger tours the United States as well as England, and she has appeared on Comedy Central. As a comedic actress, she has performed in critically acclaimed productions in New York City, San Francisco, and Washington, D.C. "I'm falling back on comedy!" she squeals. "Who knew?"

once upon a time . . .

Lesbians have come a long way; we are now talking about *paternity* instead of *patriarchy.*

When I turned thirty, my lover, Liz, asked me if I wanted to have children. "I don't know," I replied, "but I think we should keep trying!" (Why is she asking *me*, I wonder, when I could ask *her* the same question?!)

At least it opens up the deliberation, as though we could conceive by accident without some forethought and planning. "Oops, honey, the strip is blue" . . . or "red" . . . or "lavender" (whichever one indicates that you have three months before you really make up your mind).

When we do attempt conception, I wonder what it's going to be like explaining to my father about the birds and the turkey basters? "You see, Dad, they give the man a jar. Many men prefer artichoke jars. Now, personally, I think a *pickle* jar would be preferable, but—well, that's just me.

"Then, Dad, they take the jar containing the man's um . . . um, his . . . you know, the *stuff*. And they wrap it in a sock to keep the contents warm. Then it's placed between the legs of the female partner and a turkey baster is used to draw in the . . . the organic fluid. Then it is dispersed into the . . . the . . . um, coochie. Simple, huh, Dad? Then she stands on her head to ensure contact. It's the beautiful act of creation!"

I'm wondering: are my childbearing hips a biological imperative? My parents ask who will take care of me as I age. I sardonically ask them the same question. Why do I want a child? Is it biology or coercion? I've gotten my period every month for eighteen years; my menses can now vote on this issue if she wants. If she loses, she's old enough to drive to the bar, or move out on her own.

Does giving birth make me a real woman? No, earning less than a man makes me a real woman.

Nieces and nephews make me crave having my own offspring. I can have somebody say, "I love you this much," with their arms fully extended. An inner child is not sufficient to squelch the desire to procreate, either. Besides, I was forced into a custody battle for my inner child; my mother didn't like the idea of her being raised by a lesbian.

There is a now a new occasion around our house. In

addition to birthdays, anniversaries, and National Coming Out Day, I simply proclaim, "*I'm ovulating today,*" which, like other holidays, causes tension, overeating, and possible Armageddon. This finally ends in tears and strategic planning for the next month. It's like grief, only different. It's lamenting the loss of a possibility, a chance, a hope. Some people procreate so that they can make others suffer. Why, I ask, when you can just as easily join the Republican Party?

I remember the graffiti of my youth: "My mother made me a lesbian." "If I give her some yarn, will she make me one, too?" If only it were that simple. Where does a lesbian get the other essential ingredient in making a baby? We have matchmakers and sperm banks; an amalgam of the two might be best. Someone gets a man and a woman together, she says she wants children, and he leaves taking everything but some responsibility. (Sorry, that's straight couples that appear on *Oprah.*)

Two "womyn" I know are spending $3,000 a month to become impregnated. They are using frozen sperm, otherwise know as cryogenic cum. They chose this method so there would not be a man in the child's life. In fact, they only want a girl. They are using artificial insemination, but I think they're still screwed up! These "womyn" should welcome the opportunity to guide a male child; fortunately, a baby boy can teach them about love, equality, and compassion. It would be ironic if they had a male child who was so in touch with his anima that he grew up to be a drag queen. Poetic justice and karma all in one!

When you tell people that you are considering mother-hood, there are thousands of men willing to donate their services. Volunteerism doesn't apply in this circumstance. An innocent trip to the café becomes a sperm-hunting expedition: "Look! He's cute, dark hair, blue eyes, black Irish, he'd be good father material! . . . Or maybe the guy who smiled at us as we came in; disposition is important as well."

For some reason, one cannot let those under consider-ation know that they are in the running:

"Bill, what did you get on your SATs?"

"That was ten years ago. Why?"

"Just asking."

Then there is the gay male friend who might be more ideologically simpatico. Surely he would admonish the child for wanting a Barbie doll: "You do not need a Barbie doll, it's a waste! Why buy clothes for a piece of plastic when *we* can play dress up?! . . . Try on these brown cov-eralls and we'll play UPS—your mothers will be soooo proud!" It's important to encourage a child's creativity.

We homos have plenty of experience raising children. Tabitha on *Bewitched* had a gay dad, and Alice of *The Brady Bunch* fame—aka Ann B. (B for butch) Davis—helped raise a brood of six.

Children of lesbians will be just like the other kids. The same old clichés will be reverberating:

"Wait till your mother gets home!"

"When do we tell the kids that their grandparents are straight?"

"Uncle Gary will show you how to French-braid your hair, honey."

"OK, who put the empty soy-milk carton back in the fridge?"

"Mung bean casserole *again?!*"

Children of lesbian moms have the same right to be proud of their lineage and get to know their family history. "Once upon a time, there was Auntie Sarah, who dated your Mommy Suzy. Then Auntie Sarah started dating Mommy Liz on the side. After Mommy Suzy broke up with Auntie Sarah, she moved in with Auntie Karen. Auntie Karen dumped Mommy Suzy for Auntie Sarah, so your Mommy Suzy and Mommy Liz could get together and create you."

Who knew all that heartache was just nature's way of providing us with an extended family of loving babysitters?

monica
palacios

In 1982, Monica Palacios—a novice comic at the time—heard about the Valencia Rose and decided to check it out. "I'll go and just observe," she recalls thinking. "I wasn't going to say that I'm a lesbian onstage. I mean, there was no need to start a riot!" The visit, however, did incite Palacios to punch up her act with a more personal perspective.

Almost immediately, she was onstage at the Valencia Rose as an out lesbian comic. "I was hooked," she declares. "I felt really safe. I could say anything, as opposed to when I performed at the straight clubs." In addition to performing as a solo artist, Palacios also teamed up with Marga Gomez; the two collaborated as performing partners at the Rose for about two and a half years.

Branching out, Palacios entertained at various events geared to a Latino audience. At these venues, she says, "I never did my lesbian stuff because I knew they'd have a hard time with it.

Latinos have problems with homosexuality because most of the people I'm talking about are Catholics, and Catholicism condemns homosexuality." Palacios, incidentally, attended an all-girls Catholic school. "That's where I got my training," she quips.

With five years' experience as an out lesbian comic, she relocated to Los Angeles and halfheartedly dragged herself to a mainstream comedy club. "I'm here. I guess I should try it," she says flatly, setting the scene. "I walked into the club and the bouncer practically pounced on me, saying that he couldn't believe I was a comic because I was so pretty, and he asked me where I was from. I told him San Francisco, and he asked, 'Oh, are you gay?' I said, 'No.' "

Palacios pauses, visibly shaken. She continues, "I'm thinking, 'I cannot believe I just said that.' I'd been performing out comedy all those years—telling lots of people that I'm gay—but I couldn't tell this one guy that I'm gay?"

Her hunch was confirmed: "The comedy club scene is just not my thing! Comedy clubs have an aggressive atmosphere. It was because of that awful evening that I thought, 'This is not conducive to what I want to do.' " That's when she wrote *Latin Lezbo Comic,* a one-woman show that she has performed nationwide, including an off-Broadway stint at the New York Theatre Workshop.

"She works to promote positive images of lesbians, gays, Latinos, people of color, and women," Palacios's bio states. "The time has come to educate the public that these special groups are powerful, and Monica Palacios wants to be part of the teaching wave from the shores of California."

from *latin lezbo comic*

I was at a point in my life where I was getting into relationships and I was getting out of them. Finally I declared: no more commitments! No more compromises! Couples are stupid! I just want to be *Don Juanita!*

Hey, mamacita, let me touch those chi-chis!

And just when I was about to conquer *las mujeres*—the babes, those little gazelles—I met a woman at a party. There were people all around. Breasts everywhere. But when I shook her hand, it felt like we were the only ones in that room.

"Hi, my name is Monica Palacios . . . I make a decent amount of money . . . I'd like to have sex with you—*please!*"

And within a month, we were married. It just happened. No invitations were sent out. No one told us to kiss the bride. I just knew she was the woman I wanted to spend the rest of my life with. And . . . she had a gold card. Not just any gold card. Citibank gold card.

We even do typical married things. When we go to restaurants, I have to ask her for guidance: "Honey, what do I like? What's my name? Where do I live?"

It became time for *my wife—the Mrs., the little woman*—to meet my family, because I love them very much. We're very close. And, well, I thought while I'm there I could do my laundry.

We all decided on a Sunday dinner but we stumped everybody about what to make for dinner because my wife and I are strict vegetarians. My family was confused.

"What? You don't eat meat? And you don't eat chicken, fish, or cheese?! Well then, what do you eat? *What do you eat?!*"

Finally, after many calls and much, much research, we all decided on . . . Mexican food. Ooooh, that was tough. The day arrives and they are all excited to meet her. The nieces and nephews all run up to me.

"Auntie Monica, Auntie Monica, we've missed you! You don't eat chicken, fish, or cheese?! What do you eat?! *What do you eat?!*"

Of course, my precocious niece—the smart aleck!—started in on me.

"Auntie Monica, why don't you have a husband? Why are you a vegetarian? Why are you and *your friend* wearing the *same rings?!*"

So, of course, I just kind of pushed her out of the way . . . and kicked her!

My dad was playing the piano and singing away. He was singing "You Are My Sunshine," but he somehow changed the lyrics to "You don't eat chicken, fish, or cheese?!"

Finally, the time was right. I gathered everybody around the room and I said, "My family—*mi familia*—this is my wife!'' Everybody stopped talking. Dad stopped singing. After a moment of thick, intense silence, my mom says: "Come on, everybody, let's eat. Food is getting cold. C'mon, *andale*. C'mon, get the baby. Where's the baby?''

You see, they know, but they don't want to talk about it. What for? Why ruin a good meal?! And I know what they're all thinking . . .

My mom: "We know that you are . . . but we don't want to know again! Pass the butter!''

My dad: "She's not married. She brings a woman to family functions.'' Then I'm sure in his mind he's singing "Que Sarà, Sarà.''

My older sister: "Well, I don't approve of it. But she is my baby sister. At least her girlfriend is pretty—thank God!''

My older brother: "I guess she knows what she's doing. We just won't talk about it. And she better not try to hit on my wife!''

My other older sister: "I'm not sure I understand it. Her girlfriend is nice—I guess that's what she calls her. Her woman? Her lover-person?''

My little brother: "Hey, man, she can do what she wants. It's her business. She seems happy. *Oh my God! I think my wife is flirting with her girlfriend!*''

And my precocious niece: "LEZBO!!!''

But what a big burn on my family, because another older sister is *also* lesbian! You know my family thinks, "How does this happen? Did you two eat the same thing?''

Coming soon to a theater near you: "Just when the

Mexican Catholic family thought they had one lesbian daughter, they actually have two! Experience their confusion in *Double Dyke Familia!*"

Having a lesbian sister has made my life peaceful, believe me. She's always been a great role model. And about our family—well, we could never take them to a movie called *Rodeo Girls in Bondage and Birkenstocks.* But we remain connected, and that's important to me. It's the other relatives who make me crazy—you know, the ones that never encourage their daughters to say hello to me because they think I'm going to hypnotize them!

"You are getting sleepy . . . very sleepy . . . and when you wake up, you will want the love of another woman . . . and you will *not* want to eat meat—no chicken, fish, or cheese!"

karen
ripley

The familiar saying goes, "You're not getting older, you're getting better." In the case of Karen Ripley, she's also getting funnier. "I'm too tired to have a midlife crisis," says the fortysomething-year-old comic in her trademark deadpan delivery. "I'm not really deadpan," she corrects; "I'm overmedicated."

Ahead of her time, Ripley first experimented as an out lesbian comic at a coffeehouse in Berkeley in 1977, several years before the beginning of the Valencia Rose. At the time, she was six months clean and sober. "I wanted to do stand-up all along, but I was just too afraid," she says. She describes the period of her early sobriety as "a new burst of energy, a gift of being set on the right path." She often incorporates "clean and sober" humor into her act as a way to carry a message: "You know you've had too much to drink when you're hit by a parked car!"

Another rich topic for Ripley is Berkeley, where she's based.

Raised in Richmond, "just ten miles down the road," she says her relocation was like entering another world. "The first thing you have to do is get your astrological chart done," she instructs. "And throughout the eighties there was sandbox therapy and color therapy and therapy therapy," she says, her voice trailing and her eyes rolling. "It's definitely *the* mental Mecca."

While she jests about therapy and support groups onstage, Ripley candidly shares that she benefited from a phobia group when she was suddenly faced with an unusual fear—the fear of bridges. It was particularly problematic for an entertainer on a roll with gigs awaiting in San Francisco, on the other side of the Bay Bridge! Fortunately, Ripley says, she's worked through the fear: "It's been lifted. The fear was just a big imaginary wall of *ca-ca!* But, boy, it looked so real at the time!"

Ironically, the number one fear of the general population is getting up and speaking in front of a large group of people. But, says Ripley, "That one doesn't get to me so much. I like it up there onstage."

Now that the interest in openly lesbian and gay comics has caught up to speed with the veteran out comic, Ripley is finding herself performing on stages on the other side of the Bay Bridge —and way beyond. "I feel like I'm on my way now," she says. "I can call different cities and say, 'I swear to God, I'm funny, please hire me. And I can come and do this and not be a terrified child; I'm a mature adult now.' "

In fact, she welcomes her maturity in every sense. Ripley sees her career—like the careers of so many other character actresses—ripening with age. "I want to be famous when I'm really old—a dirty old lady!" she says, finally cracking a hint of a smirk. "Then I'll make big bucks. The rest of this is the journey."

i'm just a channel

In 1977, I decided to do gay and lesbian jokes because I didn't ever want to be rich and famous. It's working. Of all the careers in the world, I think of lesbian comic! But now I'd like to make more money, so I'm thinking maybe I'll pretend I'm straight. I'll get some high heels, a dress, and a push-up Wonderbra—yeah!—and I'll go perform in the Midwest. The audience will take one look and wonder, "Who's the *dyke* in the dress?"

Which brings up a question: is it OK to hate men and dress just like them?

* * *

I came out to a straight friend and told her that I'm a lesbian. The very first thing she said to me was: "Really?! Do you know Jill McGee? She's a lesbian in Philadelphia!"

Pardon me for laughing, but straight people are so funny! They think we all know each other! Actually, I *do* know her. But, hey, it's just a coincidence!

* * *

I went shopping at the women's crafts fair—gifts made by and for women. Great stuff! I got a labia earring . . . a vulva ear cuff . . . and some vagina candles.

I particularly like the vagina candles—except when you light them, they heat up and flood themselves out!

* * *

I'm from Berkeley, where I've come to learn that I'm just a channel. So it's OK with me if you don't like my jokes—God's not always that funny.

In Berkeley a lot of lesbians are environmentally sensitive. Now they have their own scent-free dances—this is the truth!—no cologne, no hair products, no deodorant. I went to one of the dances but I didn't dance with anyone—the b.o. was so bad I had to leave!

There's a lot of therapists in Berkeley, too. For a while, I went to a radical feminist therapist, whose business card stated her specialty: REICHIAN—GESTALT—DEEP TISSUE FOOT REFLEXOLOGY WITH AN EMPHASIS ON POLARITY AND CHIROPRAC-TIC—ESALEN DREAM WORK IN A SANDBOX FOR CLEAN AND SOBER QUEERS. Then I stopped and went to Richmond, where I grew up, and I joined a bowling league. I feel a lot better now. Except, today I feel a little sick to my stomach. When I wasn't looking, my inner child ate a can of Play-Doh.

* * *

Yeast infections are no fun, and it's proven that hot soap and water won't kill the virus that causes yeast. Well, I heard that a doctor on TV said, "Put your underwear in your microwave and nuke it for five minutes. This should kill the virus. So I did. Then I jumped into the shower, and my roommate came home and ate my underwear!

Then she had the nerve to tell me my crepes were tough!

I went shopping to buy feminine protection. I decided on a thirty-eight revolver.

What? You *expect me* to beat the creeps off with a *douche bag?!*

* * *

I renewed my driver's license, and on the form it asked, "Do you want to donate your organs?" I thought, "Cool. If there are some good ones, they can have them. Except my right hand and my clitoris." 'Cause you just don't know.

Admit it, you *think* you know where you're going when you die, but you don't really *really* know! You might get there and go, "Oh, shit! I gave it away!" OK, I know, it's a silly joke—there's no such operation as a *clitotomy*. But what if there was?! Imagine if you could get 'em sewn anywhere on your body! I'd get a clitoris on each fingertip and take up word processing!

Oooohhh!!

I called one of those phone-sex lines. I dialed 976-HERS, just for gals. My ex-lover answered. It was just like old times: she came, we fought about the cats, and I paid for the sex.

My friends think I'm getting fat around my waist. The truth is I'm a surrogate. I'm carrying a fibroid tumor for a woman who can't have one.

I was depressed one day so I called the suicide prevention hot line, and I'll be damned—they have voice mail!

"If you're gonna kill yourself right away, push 1 . . .

"If it can wait thirty minutes, push 2 . . .

"Out of Prozac? Push 3."

It's so easy to abuse things in our lives. I admit I abuse punctuation. I started to overpunctuate when I was small. I was afraid I'd lose my hyphen. Then I missed a few periods. I sought help; I went to an *accupunctuationist*. But things are much better now . . . now that I've discovered colon therapy.

I read in the newspaper that a big earthen dyke crumbled in Utah.

Don't laugh. I knew her.

romanovsky
& phillips

Any couple knows that a road trip can be the ultimate test of a relationship. But what would it be like traveling *and* working with an *ex*-lover?

"We had many scenes where we were pulling over to the side of the road and jumping out of the car!" says Ron Romanovsky of the popular New Mexico–based singing comedy duo Romanovsky & Phillips. "Major drama!" concurs Paul Phillips. "We never knew from one day to the next when anger or jealousy or rage or hurt was going to rear its ugly head and start another big commotion."

Their professional association began in 1982 at the Valencia Rose. Their history as lovers is less clear-cut. "We were boyfriends before we started performing, then we were lovers for seven years, then we broke up," explains Phillips. "But we kept touring."

The pair considered breaking up the act, but, says Romanovsky, "We have no other skills." So the show went on.

"At times when we were alone together, traveling, it tended to feel like the old days," Romanovsky states. "It was very confusing; we were trying *not* to be lovers." He says it was particularly confusing when they'd work together on a song. "The creative process for me—when it's really good—has a feeling that's very similar to being in love."

"The other one gets excited about it, then the next thing you know you're staying up till two o'clock in the morning, working out this new song," Phillips interjects. "That can be as good as a good orgasm!"

"We'd have those moments when we were really into the intimacy of it," says Romanovsky, "and suddenly my relationship with some other guy would seem so shallow by comparison —and it *was!*"

In an interview for a 1994 magazine article, Phillips reported they were back together as a couple: "We're once again redefining our relationship—like the two lesbians that we are!" In a follow-up article a year later, however, Romanovsky shared that the on-again, off-again relationship was off again: "We need to have a daily report, like the weather: 'R&P are apart today, but with increasing intimacy expected tonight.' "

While they're constantly redefining their relationship, they're also redefining gay entertainment. "As we travel around the country, we see people being very excited about the gay and lesbian cultural revolution that's happening—the comics, the openly gay and lesbian characters on TV—and I don't think prevolution is too strong a word," says Romanovsky. "This is going to do a lot more to impact people's perception of gay people than all the parades and marches—more than everything we've been doing for over twenty-five years since Stonewall. It's the visibility of gay and lesbian performers that really reaches people's hearts, and it allows them to be open to accepting us." Reaching a wider audience has always been an R&P goal. "I want to do a Las Vegas act—an act that a Midwestern couple would come see when they want to do something really outrageous!" Romanovsky announces. "I actually think that our act has a certain Midwestern wholesomeness." In the meantime, Romanovsky & Phillips continue to spread their wholesomeness on the road.

the homosexual agenda and functional illiteracy

ron: We get to have quite a perspective on things, because we travel to so many places. And while the gay rights movement has certainly come a long way in the past decade, the propaganda that the radical right is always spouting is so far from the reality. Like, they're always talking about the homosexual agenda . . .

paul: . . . as if queers could agree on *anything* for one minute!

ron: I always picture millions of little memo pads on the refrigerators of homosexuals throughout the land, marked "Queer Things to Do Today." And another thing, they're always talking about special rights. I mean, we do deserve *some* special rights—like parking. Just some little pink triangles next to the handicap spaces, that's all I'm asking for. My life's been a little difficult, and that would help.

paul: But what bugs me the most about these people is that they always talk as if they *own* God. So to that end, we'd like to put our two cents into this discussion.

if there is a god

I've been around the block,
I've seen a lot of sights,
From the outback of Australia
To Alaska's northern lights,
And I have to say I'm so impressed
With the beauty of this earth,
And I have a theory to impart
For whatever it is worth.
Just think about the things you've seen,
The mountains and the oceans and the prairies in
    between,
Oh, people, can't you see?
It's obvious to me
That if there is a God, He's a queen.

Drive through the Canyonlands
And you, too, will believe,
'Cause there are color combinations
That no straight man could conceive.

The striations and the textures
You will see there in the land
Could have only been invented by
A nelly holy man.

Now the Bible says He did it all within a week,
And I'm quite impressed though I've got a small
    critique:
He should not have taken that seventh day of rest
'Cause He could have done a little more work on the
    Midwest!
(At least Ohio!)

Stroll through New England
When autumn's in full force
To confirm my reference to the sexual preference
Of the one we call the Source.
And if you think I need more evidence
To really validate my claim,
What about the guy who wrote "for purple
    mountains majesty
Above the fruited plain"?

It appears we've solved one mystery
Of the earth and its creator:
Jesus might have been a carpenter,
But his father was a decorator.

* * *

paul: A little while back the federal government released a study—which they paid $15 million for—which found that 50 percent of all Americans are functionally illiterate.

ron: Now this doesn't mean that they can't read or write. Functional illiteracy means that you don't know what to *do* with what you read or write.

paul: It's like those logic problems that we used to hate in high school, remember those? You know the ones, like: "Bill has sixteen apples. If he eats three, how long will it take him to get to Detroit?"

So I've already begun developing a gay and lesbian literacy program, and I've started writing the problems for this program. Like this one: "Mary and Kay are lovers. Mary has six ex-lovers, Kay has four ex-lovers. How many best friends do Mary and Kay have?"

And here's my favorite one: "Bruce just graduated from State University of New York with a master's degree in theater arts and a double minor in music and dance. Having spent the summer understudying the role of the Windmill in *Man of La Mancha* at a small dinner theater on Long Island, he now resides in Greenwich Village. What is Bruce's current occupation?"

ron: That's right—*waiter!*

paul: You know, I'm really not making fun of the functionally illiterate among us, because I have my own areas of illiteracy and it's not necessarily funny. Like the first time I picked up a baseball bat—I *twirled* it!

what kind of self-respecting
faggot/politically correct
lesbian am i?

Guess that I was destined
To be the kind of guy
Who never really fits in
And never keeps in time.
So now I've started asking
The question on my mind:
What kind of self-respecting faggot am I?

I moved to San Francisco,
It seemed the place to be.
But I'm not into disco
And bars intimidate me.
My only can of Crisco
Is where it's supposed to be.
What kind of self-respecting faggot am I?

Don't own a single record
By Barbra, Bette or Judy.
Heard of Bette Davis,
But never saw her movies.
Guess I'm irresponsible,
It seems I've shirked my duty.
What kind of self-respecting faggot am I?

Don't have the nerve to pierce my nipples.
Don't hang out in the leather bars and pose.
Don't own a single thing from International Male.
I've not seen any Broadway shows.

I don't brunch on Sundays.
I've never ACTed UP.
My life is rather mundane
From lack of shacking up.
I even drive a Hyundai,
I guess that wraps it up.
What kind of self-respecting faggot am I?

I've never learned to two-step.
Don't spend my mornings pumping at the gym.
And if I happened to meet RuPaul on the street
Don't know what I would say to him.

So please be understanding,
It's hard to be a fag
Whose only sense of camping
Involves a sleeping bag.
Forgive me if I'm ranting,
But it's really quite a drag.
What kind of self-respecting faggot am I?

I like wearing dresses,
Don't care for Birkenstocks,
I'm not a vegetarian,
And this may be a shock:
I sometimes use a dildo
That looks just like a . . . rooster.
What kind of politically correct lesbian am I?

What kind of self-respecting homos are we?

danny
williams

Does Danny Williams object to being labeled a gay comic? The question sends him wiggling to the edge of his seat. "Of *course* I'm a gay comic! And back when I was a file clerk, I was a gay file clerk!" he says with a giddy chuckle. "If I never work again as a comic, I'm still going to be queer—I'm just going to be an *unemployed* queer!"

Williams admits that he never expected to make a living as an openly gay performer back in the early eighties, when he recorded "Castro Boy"—sort of a gay answer to Moon Zappa's "Valley Girl"—which sold about thirty thousand copies. But since 1989, he's been working a steady gig as the MC of RSVP Cruises, a gay cruise line. In addition to performing onstage, Williams is also on hand to introduce a variety of activities, from bingo to pool games. "I'm everywhere on the ship. If you orgasm, I'm there to introduce it!"

On his very first cruise, Williams knew that this was the job for him when he witnessed an unlikely pairing: a six-foot-three West Hollywood blond stud approached a dentist from Mexico City ("the nelliest human I'd ever seen in my life") and whisked him off to the dance floor. "You get on a ship with eight hundred gay people, and in about twenty-four hours, family happens," he says.

"Now, I'm really clear about what I like doing and what I don't like doing, and where I want to go with my career," says Williams. More specifically, he has little interest in pursuing spots at mainstream comedy clubs, where, in the past, he has performed alongside straight comics who solicit laughs with fag jokes.

However, Williams acknowledges that it's widely considered better to have made it in the mainstream than to have made it in the gay community. "There's a bizarre internalized homophobia in our community," he says. He remembers the sudden response when *The San Francisco Chronicle* ran a feature article about the Valencia Rose's Gay Comedy Night: "It was sold out, you couldn't get in. It was all these gay people, who I'm certain knew about it, but it wasn't until the straight press said that it was good that they thought it must be good."

He's also disappointed that major gay and lesbian events— like the opening and closing ceremonies of 1994's Gay Games IV—commonly feature straight headliners. Opines Williams, "It would be like the NAACP's award ceremony featuring all white people performing and saying, 'You know, African-Americans are really cool.' "

Finally nestling comfortably into his chair, he sighs and adds, "I'm really happy where I am now, performing essentially for the gay community." While there are some performers who adamantly demand being called a comic who *happens* to be gay, Williams says, "I think of myself as a gay man who *happens* to be a comic."

onstage

common ground

I was raised in Phoenix by very conservative parents. To this day, my mother still calls herself Mrs. Donald Williams. I try to picture her at parties. "Hi, my name is Mrs. Donald Williams, but you can call me Don."

My parents were Pentecostal. Even as a small child, I just couldn't fit in. Everybody else in the church was talking in tongues. I was *dishing* in tongues.

Of course, I was in Boy Scouts. Today, the Boy Scouts say that you can't be gay and be a member. Apparently, things have changed since I was a kid. I looked forward all year to camping, where I would spend my days doing leather crafts. I was the first scout in my troop to make a sling and a harness. Every camping trip I went on, the boys all fooled around. Straight kids lasted about a year. Gay kids went on to Eagle.

When I realized that I was gay, I told my father and he completely lost it. "Oh my God," he said, "who's going to carry on the family name?"

"But, Dad, our name is Williams. I don't think it's going to be a problem. Somebody else will do it."

* * *

Do you remember the first time you went to a gay bar? Remember wanting to be gay anyway after going to it? There is some unwritten rule that says that the first gay bar you go to has to be the worst gay bar in the universe. Everybody looks tough and carries a knife. And the bar is on the end of a pier. I lived in *Phoenix,* and the bar was on the end of a pier. It was called Jim's Steak House. It had a huge parking lot but nobody parked there because the police would come by every night and write down your license plate number and list you in their computer as a *homosexual!* I didn't care. I parked there all the time. The car was registered in my father's name. You should see the mail he gets now.

Even with my conservative background, it's still hard for me to understand why people from the far right don't like lesbians and gay men. I know why we don't like *them,* I just don't understand how they can dislike *us.* Maybe it's because we're just not real to them.

They don't see enough of us on TV. And they should. And I don't mean Richard Simmons. When straight people ask me if Richard Simmons is gay, I say, "Absolutely not. He's one of yours. I'm un-outing him. He can Deal-A-Meal, you can deal-with-him. I don't want to."

Television would be so much better if we were a constant part of it. A perfect example is the stupidest show on television, *Family Feud.* On this show, they interview straight people and then get the straight contestants to try and guess what the straight people said. I say that's too easy. I think they should interview gay men and lesbians, and get the straight contestants to guess what we think.

"We've surveyed a hundred leathermen, top five answers on the board. Name a lubricant."

"Uh, uh, uh . . . Cool Whip?"

"Number two answer, very good!"

I think our invisibility in the media is why the far right was able to demonize us in the discussion of gay men and lesbians in the military. If they don't want us in the military, then I say that straight men can't be florists and straight women can't be UPS drivers. There are so many strange rules about us being in the military. One says that you can be gay, and you can go to bars, but you can't go home with anyone. This means that most nights, I qualify for the military.

I've never been very successful in bars—especially *crowded* bars—because I'm short. A short person in a crowded bar looks like a place to stand. A little hole that travels around the bar.

Fortunately, I have a lover. We've been together for fifteen years. And that's fifteen *consecutive* years.

A straight friend asked me, "Danny, when do gay men

celebrate their anniversary? Is it the night you first met the night you first kissed, the night you first made love, or the night you moved in together?''

"Yes."

*   *   *

For years, my lover and I lived in the suburbs. Our next-door neighbors were Jehovah's Witnesses. Pretty much who I would pick to have as neighbors, right? They thought nothing of coming to my house with their copies of *Watchtower* and *Awake* and telling me to live my life like they did. I never went to their house and said, "Here's a copy of *Drummer*. I want you to have your nipples pierced by tomorrow."

When we lived in the suburbs, at least once a week the doorbell would ring at seven in the morning. I'd open the door and there would be the next-door neighbors, Hezekiah and Bathsheba. "Hi," they'd say, "we're here to share some good news with you."

"You're moving? My, that *is* good news!"

"No. We know what's missing in your life, and we're going to take you to him."

"You know Brad Pitt? All right, let's party!"

At this point, they would say something sweet and Christianlike, like "You're going to hell!"

It's not hard for me to picture gay hell. "The wind messed up my hair. There's no mousse? No blow-dryer? This is *hell!* There's nothing on TV but *Hee Haw*. My furniture's all from Levitz. I'm living in a trailer park. I'm in Colorado Springs. *Aaaaaah!!*"

* * *

My lover and I have moved back to San Francisco. He's a lawyer. If you come to San Francisco, you may see his business cards:

> SLIP AND FALL,
> GIVE US A CALL.

I am so happy to be with my lover. And, of course, there are certain changes that do happen as the years go on. I'm going to tell you a true story, then I'd like you to guess which of the following two things my lover of fifteen years said to me.

We have a teapot (from Williams-Sonoma, of course), and as I was pouring boiling water from the teapot to a cup, the lid fell off the teapot, which caused my arm to be scalded. Did my lover of fifteen years say:

(a) "Oh my goodness, darling, you've burned your arm. My, that must hurt. Sit down whilst I get some salve and bandages, my sweetheart."

or . . .

(b) "You never put the lid on tight enough. I told you to put the lid on tightly, but you never listen. What do you mean, where's the salve? You had it last. You never put things away where they're supposed to go."

This test works equally well if you're gay or straight. I think that we have a lot more in common than most people think. If you're straight, I'd like to ask you some questions:

1. How old were you when you first realized you were straight?

2. Growing up, particularly during adolescence, did you have unexplainable feelings, and did you feel like you were the only one?

3. Have you told your parents yet that you're straight?

You see, we do have so much in common.

meanwhile, in the eighties on the east coast . . .

Just as one needn't be Jewish to enjoy that particular brand of rye bread, one needn't be a lesbian to enjoy the humor of Kate Clinton, one of the first openly gay women to make it big on the stand-up circuit.

—Tom Jacobs, *Daily Variety*

Much of Jaffe Cohen's humor is in the tradition of borscht-belt comedy . . . his gayness gives it a fresh spunkiness.

—Anthony Tommasini, *The Boston Globe*

[Lynn Lavner is] a fabulous entertainer . . . someone with whom I've shared bagels and lox.

—Harvey Fierstein

Danny McWilliams is delicious as he offers up various character types. . . . McWilliams' delivery is quick, sharp . . . always a scream.

—Martin Schaeffer, *The New York Native*

kate
clinton

What advice does Kate Clinton have for someone who's coming out? "The only thing I know," she says, "is don't come out to your dad in a moving vehicle!" When Clinton came out, she was shunned by her family. "Thinking back, I kind of liked it," she admits. "Now, they come and visit!"

A former high school teacher from Syracuse, New York, Clinton has been performing as an out comic for a long time. "Since before lesbians were invented," she deadpans. Actually it's been since 1981. "A lot of Unitarian church basements," she says, recalling her early gigs, which also included women's coffeehouses and music festivals. Relocated to Provincetown, Massachusetts, her stage outing immediately became a big hit with the gay resorts' visitors.

Now Clinton is coming out to an ever-expanding audience. Her one-woman show, *Out Is In,* enjoyed a successful run off-Broadway, and she made Arsenio Hall blush when she told his national TV audience, "Some people wouldn't know a lesbian if their mouth was full of one!" Ironically, those racy words came from the individual *The Los Angeles Times* called "the kind of lesbian you can take home to your parents." While Clinton emphasizes that she has "a very radical heart," she acknowledges her wholesome image: "I can't get past looking like a Campbell Soup kid."

She also appeared on Comedy Central's *Out There II,* which aired on National Coming Out Day in 1994. Backstage at Caroline's Comedy Club in New York, just prior to the taping of the show, Clinton mischievously mused, "I like to celebrate National Coming *On to* Day. That's when you choose a straight person and you just go for it! Like, you pick your bank teller, make your plan, then just come on to her!" Or, she suggests, we could celebrate National *In-ing* Day. "When people come out that we don't really like, we can say, 'No, *you* keep him!' "

Clinton gratefully salutes the network of women cultural workers that flourished in the seventies. "During most of that time, I was *just* to the left of Newt Gingrich," she says. "Then I listened to [women's] music and I was transformed. And through that transformation, I began to do the political work that I do now."

From church basements to national television, Clinton says the work she does—both cultural and political—"still feels important." And, she says, "as a teacher I know that you need to repeat things and repeat things and repeat things, and you need to say it in a bunch of different ways until everyone finally hears it: that it's OK to be gay and to come out."

Has her family gotten the message? "Now we're so comfortable with each other, they like to stay for two weeks," says Clinton, who used to "de-dyke" her place for parental visits, for example, hide books with the word "lesbian" on the cover. "Now I leave things out to try to drive them away!"

holy apologies

September 1995: The other day, in the mail, with my very pretentious J. Peterman catalogue and my Publishers Clearinghouse notice thanking me for sending Ed McMahon the map to my house so he will better be able to find me on that great prize-awarding day, I got a letter from the pope. I was at first overwhelmed by his thoughtfulness. Then I found out he had sent a letter to every woman. But still. And I did appreciate the Nixon stamp—an inspired bit of whimsy.

It wasn't one of those pray-or-else chain letters, one of those "Don't be like Mrs. Eulah Banks, of Okra, North Carolina, whose husband fell into the moving trash compactor on the back of his self-owned garbage truck after she delayed her reply" things. It was a letter of apology. Talk about your letter bombs! Lately it seems as if everybody is apologizing. Well, everybody but O.J.

Lots of religions are apologizing for things. I guess they are not sleeping well. Recently eight hundred German Christians apologized to some baffled Danes for the Nazi invasion of the Netherlands. In the United States, the Southern Baptist Convention formally and finally apologized to African Americans for defending slavery in the antebellum South and for condoning contemporary racism. African Americans everywhere were relieved. They'd been waiting. Go get out your Tracy Chapman album and crank up "Sorry is all that you can say" to window-rattling decibels.

In this letter of apology, entitled *Ego Sum Okay, Vos Estis Excommunicatae*, the Pope apologized for any (?!) injustices against women in the name of the Roman Catholic Church. The Jesuits had earlier apologized for abetting centuries of male domination and had pledged their personal solidarity with women, frightening many coeds at Boston College.

But there is no "Why now?" to this papal apology. Upon receiving the apology, I note the U.N. Conference on Women is about to convene in Beijing and His Extreme Cleverness is trying to *carp* the *diem*. All that true-nature-of-women talk in his apology makes this lesbian suspect that a few hundred years from now, some Pope John Paul LXXXVI is going to be apologizing for that unfortunate crusade against women in the late 1900s.

Supposedly, all these apologies for past sins are necessary before the Vatican can send out party invites to the third millennium of Christianity. Well, excuse me for being such a party pooper, but talk is cheap, and whatever happened to good old penance?

The Southern Baptists should have to create jobs in city

centers and work for the defeat of Jesse Helms. And the Vatican should accept my low bid to produce the two-thousandth-birthday bashes throughout the country. You thought the Tall Ships were big. It's several years off, but I am planning now.

They know me at the Vatican already for some of the bids I have put in to produce papal visits. I proposed hooking the pope up with the Lollapalooza tour awhile back. Push the miracle thing. Kind of a Neil Young thing, get the younger crowd. He's got the book, the CD, lots of merch, and a very good road show.

And I've been trying to talk Mary into coming back. She does not like big events. She likes small appearances. Backyards. Lawn chairs. New Jersey. Nothing too showy. I like that about her. She's like Jackie O. in that way.

If the Vatican accepts my bid, I'll think about taping my picture of the pope back together.

jaffe
cohen

"If I wasn't gay, I'd be just one more little Jewish comic with glasses," declares Jaffe Cohen, playfully peering over his wire rims. "I find it so strange when I hear people hiding the fact that they're gay, because when I discovered I was gay, my reaction was, 'Oh, good—*subject matter!* I have something to talk about and write about. I have a perspective that I can bring to my art.' "

Cohen began performing as a stand-up comic in 1986, "the year after Rock Hudson died, so there was a lot of homophobia and AIDS phobia," he notes. "By then I was already in my thirties, my activism was already in place, my gay identity was already very strong; there was no way I was going to start lying about myself at that point." Actually, a primary reason Cohen became an openly gay comic was in response to AIDS: "I'd seen my friends get sick and die, and my appreciation of life at that point was that nothing was going to stop me from having a great time with my career and doing whatever the fuck I wanted to do. And when I first started going onstage, I was thinking, 'This may be scary, but being put on a respirator at Saint Vincent's was a hell of a lot scarier for friends of mine.' That gave me a level of fearlessness."

For the next couple of years, Cohen braved the comedy club circuit around the boroughs of New York—not the ideal audience for his act at that particular time, he found. Deducing that his target audience was theatergoers—gay or straight ("Straight people go to the theater; they've seen *Torch Song Trilogy*")—Cohen envisioned a gay stand-up comedy collective, suitable for a theater-cabaret setting. In 1989, he invited Danny McWilliams and Bob Smith to join him, and collectively they became Funny Gay Males. A two-week engagement at the Duplex cabaret in Greenwich Village turned into an unprecedented two-year run. The trio appeared on several television shows, including *The Joan Rivers Show*, on which Rivers praised them as "comic pioneers." At about the same time, Cohen also took pioneering steps as one of the first solo artists to perform openly gay material on network television when he appeared on Fox's *Comic Strip Live.*

But according to Cohen, who continues to perform as a stand-up while concentrating on writing projects, you ain't seen nothing yet! "By the year 2000, I think there's going to be a flourishing of gay culture that's going to make anything we've seen in the past look like peanuts!" he predicts.

"There's a very rich literary and comic tradition in the gay community," Cohen continues. "There's a tremendous creative energy that will be unleashed, and I think we'll see more gay characters on TV and in films—and it will be more than 'the flavor of the month.' By 2000, the comedy and entertainment industries will have a very large openly gay element, somewhat similar to how stand-up comedy was a very large Jewish monopoly in the fifties and sixties. We've seen ethnicity become a part of the humor, and I think that's what will happen with gays.

"Gay humor will be very big!"

Last week I called up my ex, B.G., and we got along fabulously. He jokingly told me that he would love to see me in person so he could smack me around again for old times' sake. B.G., you see, was into rough sex. Me? I like to cuddle. B.G. could bruise me just by rolling over in bed. I, on the other hand, could pummel and pinch with all my might and B.G. hardly knew I was in the room. We had very different thresholds of pain; neurologically, we were a mixed marriage.

This, by the way, had been only one of our many problems. B.G. was also way too young for me. When we first started dating, my friends referred to me as being "with child." We also lived in two distinct cultural universes. He was a young queer and I was an old queen. Whenever I screeched happily over some ancient Bette Davis movie, B.G. would get up and leave the room. His education was incomplete. He thought that Kate Smith was one of the original Charlie's angels. He was also a quiet guy, and I found his stony expressions unsettling; it was like trying to converse with Mount Rushmore, and half the time I wasn't sure whether to kiss him or sing "Hail to the Chief."

In fact, he didn't even tell me that he was leatherman until about two months into our relationship, the night he reached underneath his bed and pulled up a dusty old satchel strangely similar to the suitcase that Julie Andrews carried in *Mary Poppins*. When he undid the latch, I half expected to see a magical hat rack levitate from within. Instead, B.G. lifted out a black leather harness with silver studs and he asked me if I wanted to try it on. Ever curious, I slipped the gear over my head and examined myself in the mirror.

"What am I supposed to do now? Plow Central Park?"

"Don't you feel more powerful now?" he asked.

"Oh, sure." I said. "Does this come in any other colors besides black?"

"Aren't you into rough sex?" B.G. asked.

"Who needs to be beat up in bed?" I said. "I'm Jewish. We get enough abuse."

We went to sleep without even attempting to have sex.

That night I had my first S&M nightmare. I dreamed that B.G. and I were getting married, and B.G., my bride-to-be, was registering a leather pattern at the Pleasure Chest. The gifts poured in, and after the wedding B.G. began decorating our house in early Spanish Inquisition.

In every room there were instruments of extreme discomfort, such as sandpaper toilet tissue and leftover noodle kugel from my aunt Mary's Passover dinner. The next thing I knew, there were three big hairy men dressed as Cossacks and they were tying me down while sneering anti-Semitic remarks. Meanwhile, B.G., wearing the black harness from the night before, had produced the ultimate instrument of Jewish torture: an old tape of Barbra Streisand's Christmas album, and I was forced to listen to Barbra singing "Little Drummer Boy" over and over until the blood started trickling out of my ears. Just then, Yassir Arafat climbed into bed with B.G. and me and suggested a threesome. I woke up with a start. B.G., meanwhile, was sleeping soundly with a smile on his face. I imagined that he was having the same dream as I was—only he was enjoying it!

The next month, B.G. suggested that we both get our nipples pierced and insert little rings into our chests. "Fabulous," I replied. "That way I would never lose my house keys." B.G. didn't laugh and hardly talked to me for the rest of the day. As the weeks wore on, he slipped further and further away from me until there was nothing I could do about it. Our incompatibility was more and more apparent. If he asked me to slap him in bed, I would slap him just like he asked me, but still he wasn't satisfied.

"You're hitting me, but your *heart* isn't in it," he said. "Make me your slave."

"You've already folded my laundry. I can't think of anything else I need."

"Don't worry about hurting me!" B.G. pleaded. "The pain increases the pleasure."

"I don't know, B.G. To me, pain and pleasure are two different things. Pain distracts from pleasure. When I was a kid, my brother would bang me in the head while I was watching *I Love Lucy*. Believe me, it didn't increase my pleasure. And another thing . . ."

"What?"

"I think it's weird the way you talk dirty in bed. You just get so serious. Your voice drops an octave. 'Yeah, baby! Yeah!' You sound like Mercedes McCambridge."

"Who?"

"Forget it."

"So what am I supposed to do to turn you on?" he finally asked.

"Kiss me. Hug me. Tell me that I'm cute and funny."

"You know, Jaffe, you just don't understand sex."

A month after that discussion, I suggested that B.G. visit a friend of his in San Diego, and—to make a long story short—he never came back. At first I was relieved that the relationship had ended without my having made a decision, but very slowly I began to be filled with self-pity. Then came the rage. If anyone even mentioned the West Coast, I would get this feeling in my chest like I'd been stabbed with a rusty fork. I became obsessed with climate conditions in southern California, and some nights I'd even stay up late, watching the Weather Channel and praying for mud slides. Obviously I was out of control. So about a year ago, I finally swallowed my pride and called

B.G. for the first time to ask him—very casually—how he was getting on.

We chatted amiably. He'd gotten a job in a video store and, strangely enough, he was finally starting to develop a taste for old Bette Davis movies.

"How wonderful!" I said. "You're growing up at last."

"Yeah, my favorite is that one where she beats up Joan Crawford and ties her up in bed."

"That figures." And then I just had to ask: "So . . . you dating anyone?"

B.G. then took a deep breath and began reciting a litany of names about as long as the distance between here and Death Valley—all names unused east of the Mississippi—Forrest, Cody, Rock, Clint. They all sounded like geographical formations, and I imagined them all to be strong and silent with hard bodies and the personalities of fence posts.

"You sound like you're having a great time!" I hissed cheerfully.

"Not really," B.G. replied. "I don't have any real friends yet, and—I miss you."

"I miss you, too."

There was a long pause on the other end. Then B.G. laughed.

"Remember the time I made you put on that heavy metal cock ring?"

"Yeah. I couldn't get it off and almost drowned the next time I went swimming!"

B.G. then explained that even though it was painful, he

still needed to be on his own. His goals were simple. He wanted to grow hair on his back, save up enough money to buy more gear for his satchel, and find more leathermen who liked what he liked in bed.

That night I slumped into bed feeling crushed and abandoned, but then, slowly, some joy started to seep in. Everything was fine, I told myself. Nothing had gone awry. B.G., my baby, was simply maturing into his own man—not like I would have expected, but he was growing up.

My heart was so full that it ached, and I knew then that I loved B.G. infinitely more than when we'd been together, and—worse—that I would never stop loving him. Ouch!!

For the first time, I realized that B.G. had been right all along. Pain does increase pleasure, and pleasure—unfortunately—never comes without pain.

lynn
lavner

If you're going to sit and schmooze over a cup of java, do it with an opinionated Brooklynite like Lynn Lavner! Broach any topic, and she shares (or, as she quips, "self-discloses") with a sharp sense of humor and a strong sense of history.

As she rummages through her bag and extracts a press kit, she gives special attention to other contents: a couple of colorful children's toys. Following the interview, Lavner explains, she's meeting with a friend's child, Nicholas. "I'm the only adult at his birthday parties, and he's the only kid at mine," she elaborates with childlike enthusiasm.

As for her own childhood, she says, "My fantasy at age three was to wear formal men's clothing and flirt with a beautiful woman by singing her a song." A few decades later, in 1982, Lavner found herself at a Greenwich Village bar, playing the piano and singing, but not to a beautiful woman—well, not exactly. "I was singing a funny little song that I wrote, and a drag queen came up to me and said, 'Do you have an hour of that?' And I said, 'Honey, I have a *lifetime* of that!' " The encounter led to a successful run at the Duplex cabaret.

"Cabaret is a very old and revolutionary art form," says Lavner, who for many years has billed herself as the World's Most Politically Incorrect Entertainer. "When cabaret started in France and Germany, it was antigovernment, antiestablishment. I like to say that if the emperor is not wearing clothes, you'll hear it first from me."

Describing her act as having "more to do with Mel Brooks than with Holly Near," Lavner notes that her early cabaret shows attracted a predominantly gay male audience. Jokes Lavner: "I cultivated a relationship with the gay male community, because I knew I might one day want to cook a meal, decorate an apartment, or go shopping!"

In 1986, she performed at the Southern Women's Festival in Georgia (along with Melissa Etheridge). "It was my first women's festival," she says, shrugging, "and they said it was alcohol-free, chem-free and drug-free. I thought, 'That's terrific! Usually you have to *pay* for that stuff!' " Now her favorite venues to perform are college campuses. "One of the real obligations that we now have as out adults, to kids and to teenagers and to young adults, is to let them know that their dreams can come true, and not to ghettoize themselves, and not to let this vicious radical-right stuff—I call it the Contract *on* America— limit their horizons."

That's a lesson Lavner hopes she's passed on to her daughters, whom she raised with her lover. "It's tough to go through childhood and adolescence, even *without* mothers who are into leather!" she says, laughing. "But we realize that the kids really got a tremendous kick out of it and loved us, and loved our 'weird and wicked' ways!"

Their kids are now grown up, and, notes Lavner, "My lover and I have raised three daughters—each one of them is straight." Fighting a giggle, she adds, "We wonder what it was that we did wrong, but we try to accept them and love them as they are!"

onstage

butch fatale

Not long ago it was my pleasure to emcee the Leaping Lesbian Follies in Denver. That's an annual show (I think they've been doing it for some fifteen years) and they bill it as "a musical review in two unnatural acts." It's really wonderful: all amateurs, except for one professional entertainer that they bring in to emcee, perform a little, and pull it together. Now, when I got there, I was really impressed because it's an all-woman production. Women book the entertainers, do the performing, the tech stuff, the backstage chores, the advertising, the promotion—and it's a women-only event. So just to be amusing, on the night of the show, somebody took down the regular restroom signs and replaced them with signs that said "Butch" and "Femme."

There were about five hundred women in the audience,

and you have never seen such a collective nervous break-down! No one knew where to go to the bathroom. Women ran out into the bushes, women ran up into mountains, women exploded in the mezzanine. It was not a pretty sight. So I realized that this is kind of a problem in some areas, and I thought that as an elder "statesdyke," I had to address it.

Now, I've been told that the ideal couple comprises a soft butch and an aggressive femme. And it's true: if you go back through history you've got Romeo and Juliet, George Burns and Gracie Allen, Warren Beatty and Warren Beatty. So I tried to talk some sense into these women who were taking it all so seriously. I told them that the way you can tell which restroom you need to use is to ask yourself a few questions. If you look in the mirror twenty minutes every morning, you are a femme. But if you look for twenty minutes in every mirror you pass all day, you are a butch.

Butches will not go shopping under any circumstances —except for sneakers. Femmes will get out of a hospital bed to go shopping. Right? And they like to buy things for their butches. They'll come home and say, "Honey, I got you a shirt." But is the butch grateful? No. The butch will look puzzled and ask, "What for? I already have a shirt." So the femme will take revenge by dragging her butch along to a department store and forcing her to sit outside the fitting rooms with all the straight husbands (and those bastards won't give you a piece of the sports section to save your life).

Wouldn't you think that if a femme is allowed to take five items into a dressing room she'll take five *different* items? Nope. A femme will take the *same* outfit in five different *sizes.* "Bring me a 6, an 8, a 10, a 12, and a 14. Maybe it runs big in the hips, short in the waist, long in the shoulders . . ." You're schlepping this stuff back and forth and back and forth. And I can tell you it's embarrassing to be a five-foot-tall, ninety-eight-pound butch. You've got a credibility problem to begin with. At home, I find myself saying things like, "Yo, woman. Reach me down the shredded wheat. Please."

But people outside the lesbian and gay community don't have any problems with this. They subliminally understand the concept of butch and femme. For instance, when I perform in a certain town, where my lover has an elderly aunt, we take her out to dinner. She will invariably give *me* her coat to hang up. I can't even *reach* the hook. And even in the most unsophisticated circumstances . . .

I was driving home from gigs in Virginia one time, and we got off the interstate. That, by the way, is not really a bright thing to do with my haircut and a New York license plate. But there we were, in a little town, and we stopped at a motel. It wasn't even Motel Six, more like Motel Four and a Half. We go into the office and the redneck husband has his feet up on the desk, he's chomping on a toothpick, and he's doing absolutely no work. His wife is running around the office and she's doing *everything:* she's checking people in, checking people out, answering the mail, answering the phone. She gives us a room, tells us where we can go for dinner, the whole thing. And just as we're about to leave the office, my lover turns to her and asks, "By the way, if we should feel like taking a walk later, is there perhaps a mall nearby?" With that, the husband spits out his toothpick in disgust, whirls around, stamps his feet down on the floor, looks directly at *me* and says, "Hmmf. If there's a place to go shopping, they'll find it, won't they?" And I think, "They? *They?*"

I whispered to my lover, "Let's get out of here before Lemuel invites me along on a turkey shoot." It was my first experience with male bonding.

a lesbian too long

I've got clothing in my closet that Rommel wouldn't
   wear,
I think I've been a lesbian too long.
Letterman won't book me, hold your breath until I
   care,
I think I've been a lesbian too long.
I never met a queen I couldn't dish with,
I never met a folk song I could stand.
The other day I realized I can spell "Margarethe
   Cammermeyer,"
I think I've been a lesbian too long.

There's absolutely nothing with batteries on my
   shelf,
I think I've been a lesbian too long.
I may not be Madonna, but I vibrate for myself,

I think I've been a lesbian too long.

There's more to life than trashing all your sisters,
Perhaps one should employ this rule of thumb:
Anything worth doing gets Patricia Ireland in
    trouble,
I think I've been a lesbian too long.

Why is there a soupçon of suspicion in my heart,
In matters of the current ruling class?
The FBI, the CIA, the NRA, the FDA,
If it's got three letters, bud, I watch my ass.
Will the INS repeal the alien fag act?
I'm Jewish, so I always keep a bag packed.

The CDC informs me that I'm safe the way I am,
They think I've been a lesbian too long.
Frankly, my dear, I don't give a dental dam,
I play safe to stay a lesbian longer.
My conscience can't be cut to this year's fashion,
The lessons of the past are far too strong.
I remember when Patty Duke was normal and there
    was something wrong with *me*,
I think I've been a lesbian too long.

It behooves me to admit k.d. lang gives me no thrill,
I think I've been a lesbian too long.
She may be de rigueur but I prefer Anita Hill.
Do you suppose it's possible that she . . . oh, never
    mind.
I'm very proud to say that I'm pro-*choices*,

That's so much more than being just pro-choice.

My prenuptial agreement was witnessed by Martina
   Navratilova's grandmother,

I think I've been a lesbian,

A well-adjusted lesbian,

A happy, healthy lesbian,

Left-handed, leather lesbian,

I'm amazed I've been a lesbian this long!

danny mcwilliams

"I had no intention of being an openly gay comic; I kind of fell into it," says Danny McWilliams, who started performing comedy in New York City in 1982. "I worked a lot of straight clubs, in front of straight crowds. I didn't do openly gay stuff, but I think they knew I was gay." While his material may not have been overtly gay, even then McWilliams used comedy to deflect the terrors of "an all-male jock Catholic high school."

Any ambiguity regarding his sexual orientation was cleared up in 1988 when McWilliams joined forces with Jaffe Cohen and Bob Smith and called themselves Funny Gay Males. The trio authored the book *Growing Up Gay,* published in 1995, and again McWilliams was able to draw upon his memories as a funny gay boy.

How do three authors write one book? "For months and months we'd get together and throw out ideas, and we laughed our asses off!" says McWilliams. "It was like *The Dick Van Dyke*

Show; we were like the three writers: Sally, Buddy, and Rob! Then came the hard part—we had to write it all down!"

The book states, " 'Vivacious' is a lovely modifier if you happen to be Liza Minnelli, but for a 7-year-old boy, you may just as well use the word 'queer,' and in most cases, you'd be right on the money." McWilliams proudly acknowledges that he was, indeed, a "vivacious" seven-year-old. It was around that age that he identified with guests on a TV special hosted by advice columnist Ann Landers. "She interviewed these gay people, and I realized that I felt like they do," he says. "But I thought they were freaks. There had to be something wrong with them—I mean, they were talking with Ann Landers!"

If you can't find solace from Ann Landers, what's a young gay boy to do? Recalls McWilliams: "When I was in the third grade, I asked my Ouija board if it was OK that I had a crush on this boy named Richard, and it said it was OK; it didn't spell out F-A-G-G-O-T!"

In high school, McWilliams found his niche—drama club! However, his theatrical talents went unappreciated at his all-jock school in Queens. With as much school spirit as he could muster, he made a grand entrance into each classroom as he hawked tickets for *Barefoot in the Park.* "These jocks threw things at me!" he laments with a mock moan, which abruptly turns into a hearty roar. "It wasn't funny then, but thinking about it now, it's funny!"

Through his humor, McWilliams hopes to project that message: "Someday you'll look back and laugh." To gay kids who are currently in similarly intimidating situations, McWilliams advises, "Ignore these idiots; they've got to pick on somebody so they don't get picked on themselves. Just be strong. When you get out of high school, believe me, things will be so much better."

onstage

▶ under my spell

I had a nun in the third grade who told me in front of the whole class that I "act like a girl." So the next day I was out sick. When I came back she asked, "Where have you been, young man?" I said, "Woman's problems."

A nun told me I was going to receive my Confirmation, so I must choose a Confirmation name, and it must be the name of a saint. So I chose Eva Marie.

I knew I was gay when I was twelve years old. My brother says to me, "Hey, Danny, look at the hooters on that babe! You know what hooters are?" I said, "I know what hooters are." He says, "Use the word 'hooter' in a sentence." I said, "Hooter hell decorated this room?"

My mother had plastic slipcovers on the couch. When I was six years old, I put a ham sandwich in it. When I found it last week, it was still fresh!

I went on *The Joan Rivers Show* as an openly gay comic. My mother was horrified that the neighbors would see. So on the show, Joan asks me, "What does your mother think of you coming on the show?" I said, "My mother is on the rooftops in Queens cutting the cable wires!"

Remember when homosexuality was considered an illness? It was fine by me. I figured, I'll go see Liza Minnelli and charge the tickets to Blue Cross and Blue Shield.

I worked a nine-to-five office job. The office manager approached me one day and yelled, "Shirt and tie!" I had on a T-shirt. She curtly repeated to me, "Shirt and tie!" I was thinking to myself, "Shirt and tie . . . shirt and tie?" *Oh!!* I yelled back, "Things you wear at a wedding! . . . Things you wear to dinner!" I love playing *$25,000 Pyramid!*

I love Court TV—especially the Menendez brothers trial. They sure are cute! I couldn't serve jury duty. I'd be like, "They killed their parents? Is there a problem?"

I wonder what I'd say to them if I saw them in person? "Eric, Lyle, I love your work!"

I called an adult party line once. A man got on the line and asked, "What do you have on?" I said, *"Bewitched."*

I thought it was great the way Endora cast her spells, like Shakespeare, on those who deserved it. I thought,

"What a great way to get revenge! Casting spells!" So one day, when I was a kid, I was in school and these two guys yelled out, "Hey, McWilliams, you're a big fag!" I pretended I was Endora, and I said, "Bat wings, cow's eyes, the moon in eclipse; make those two butch as Quentin Crisp!"

I went to Wigstock. I love drag queens. I've always wondered if drag queens practice when they're kids. And do their mothers influence them? I picture a mother yelling out the window, "Michael, did you practice your Carol Channing today?"

We need some lesbian drag queens. I wonder who they would do—Lou Grant?

Sometimes it's hard to tell if a person is a man or a woman by their names nowadays. Like, I thought Shaquille O'Neal was the young actress on *The Cosby Show.*

I like Sinead O'Connor. Remember when she tore up the picture of the pope and everyone had a fit? What was the problem? Was that the only photo they had of that guy?

We have the Meals on Wheels program in New York. But, at first, I didn't know it was for homebound senior citizens; I thought it was for anyone. So as a starving actor, I called one day and ordered the corned beef. Then I sat at my makeup table and made myself look like Rose Kennedy. *Bon appétit!*

Remember a couple of years ago in New York we had medical waste wash up on shore? Well, twenty years ago I had my appendix removed; I found it at Jones Beach! Thank God I didn't have a sex change!

late bloomers: established comics come out in the nineties

I came out professionally last year, so now I'm a professional lesbian—which means I'm really good at it!

—Amanda Bearse, hosting Comedy Central's
Out There II, October 1994

judy carter

Judy Carter wrote the book on stand-up comedy. Literally. She's the author of *Stand-Up Comedy: The Book,* which is in its fourth printing and has been featured on *Oprah, Entertainment Tonight,* and even *ABC World News.* One of the first women on the stand-up circuit, the Los Angeles–based comic began her career in 1975. She spent more than fifteen years on the road opening for everyone from Pat Boone to Prince, and she was a regular on *The Merv Griffin Show.*

"When I first started doing stand-up, I wasn't aware that I was gay," says Carter. "About five years into my comedy career, I came out in my personal life. My life changed, but my act remained the same, except that I began avoiding pronouns. Being authentic onstage has always been very important for me, so I felt really horrible."

That's when she took time off from the road and wrote the how-to primer for budding humorists. Spurred by the book's whopping success, Carter began conducting stand-up-comedy workshops. "I started teaching other people how to be who they were," she says. "I noticed that some of my students were gay but not out, and I saw that they could not tap into their creativity because every idea had to go through this self-imposed filter. And the filter doesn't just filter out that they might say something that reveals that they're gay, like saying the word 'lover' or something; the filter filters *everything*. It was really difficult for them to be their spontaneous selves, and I saw how much damage that caused." (Carter addresses these issues in her latest book, *The Homo Handbook,* a practical and humorous guide to coming out.)

After several years of teaching, she decided to return to the stage—"and I *had* to be an out lesbian," she says. Now, Carter bills herself as "just another Jewish lesbian comic-magician." In addition to tackling subjects such as lesbian relationships, political correctness, and therapy, her act includes "a death-defying escape" from her grandmother's girdle!

"What other people think of me does not run my life anymore," says Carter, "and that gives a person tremendous artistic freedom."

nice girls don't say things like that

My grandmother actually knew I was gay before I did. I really didn't know. My grandmother turned to me and—in her Yiddish accent—she says, "So, Judy, what? Are you a homosectional?"

I thought that was something you bought in department stores. "I'd like two end tables . . . and that lovely homosectional."

I didn't have a clue that one day in my bedroom, I actually *would* have a homosectional. And, you know, they *are* lovely to sit on!

I know that some lesbians are getting pregnant by going to sperm banks. I couldn't do that. I'm exactly like my grandmother. "What? Everything's *frozen?!* Nothing's *fresh?!*"

It's really courageous of people to come out at work. When you come out, you get labeled. Like if you work in an office, all of a sudden you start hearing over the intercom, "*Lesbian*, line one . . . it's your very *special* friend!"

It's so hard being gay. It's a lot easier being black than being gay. At least when you're black, you don't have to tell your parents.

All these religious people tell us we're going to hell. If we're going to hell, I'd like to see everybody in heaven try to get their hair done! Heaven will be one bad hair day after another.

Actually, Catholic girls make the best lesbians. Their whole life they're told, "Don't have sex with men—it's a sin!" They're like, "Oh, OK, I can do that!"

✳ ✳ ✳

I'm so sick of hearing about family values. Most of us are in therapy *because* of our families!

I'm surprised that you don't hear about more calls to 911: *"Help me, I'm in a family. Get me out of here!"*

I lived with my lover and we brought up her son and we were a *family*. It was just like *The Dick Van Dyke Show*. But it was more like *The Dick DYKE-DYKE Show*.

Wouldn't that be a great sitcom? "Coming to ABC! Three people . . . one wardrobe! Stay tuned!"

Lesbian TV shows would be fun. We could have *The Dykes of Hazzard*, *Desiring Women*. And for the guys, *Married with Poodles*.

✳ ✳ ✳

It's so hard to keep a relationship going in Los Angeles. L.A. is like the Land of Teflon Affairs—nothing sticks. You go on vacation with your lover, you're broken up by the time you get home. Thank God for One-Hour Photo! You can actually see your photos while you're still in the relationship. "Look how happy we are, honey . . . *Honey? Where are you going?*"

I think it's healthy for some people to break up. And some people can break up so easily, it's like, "You left your socks in the living room again. That's *it!*" And then, for other people, it's like, "You left your socks in the living room, you don't have a job, you've emptied my bank account, you've slept with my sister . . . and if it happens *again*, that's *it!*"

My therapist always says that you really should be friends with someone before you sleep with them. But the truth of the matter is, once you get to know someone, who the hell wants to have sex with them?!

Yeah, I'm in therapy. What I don't get about therapy is this: if you always pick the wrong person to be in a relationship with, what makes you think you're going to pick any better when you pick your therapist?!

My last therapist was so screwed up, she had more problems than I do! She was so fat, *she* had to sit on the couch! She was *jealous* when I got better! I told her, "I'm feeling a lot better about myself." She was like, "Well, *goody, goody, goody* for *you!*"

It's so hard to have self-esteem in our world—especially in gay bars. I'm surprised that at some of these bars they don't have age police outside. *"Hold it! You're doing forty-three in a twenty-three-year-old zone!"*

When are you *too* old? Does it just happen overnight? Do you just wake up one morning and no matter how hot it is, you *want* to wear a coat?!

*   *   *

Growing up, I always thought that I wanted to marry an athletic, rich man. And now, I'm jogging and making money. I finally became the man I thought I wanted to marry!

michael
dane

It begins as a familiar scenario: it's Saturday night at a comedy club (in this particular case, in Worcester, Massachusetts). The audience has been entertained by the host, the opening act, and the middle act. But when the headliner is introduced, we sense a deviation from the usual stand-up presentation.

"Ladies and gentlemen, please welcome to the stage . . . Michael Dane!"

Dane, however, bypasses the stage and paces alongside the front-row tables—where he'll station himself for the rest of the show. He launches into his act, sans microphone, projecting loud and clear.

Dane gives them much more than their ten bucks' worth; he gives them theater.

As he's about one third into his set, Dane instructs a group of inebriated patrons to quiet down or leave. One of the customers hurls verbal threats and lunges toward the comic. The unruly group is booted out, and the audience applauds in support of Dane's gumption. "Oh, sure, you applaud," he ad-libs, "but who's going to walk me to my car after the show?"

Instantly, a patron sitting ringside (imagine an Andrew Dice Clay look-alike on steroids) stands and good-naturedly hollers, "Who else is gonna help me walk this guy to his car?" En masse, the audience cheers. "That was all planned!" the comic jokes, and forges onward. Clearly, Dane has the crowd on his side. And, believe it or not, all this hullabaloo happens *before* the fun *really* begins! Just moments later, Dane blurts out, *"I'm bisexual!"*

Originally from Los Angeles, Dane began performing as a stand-up comic in 1983; he was "straight-identified" at the time, he says. While pursuing acting roles at regional theaters in the Midwest, Dane frequented gay-supported cabarets, "because I liked Sondheim," he says with a sagacious smirk. "It was intriguing: the same gay men who had welcomed me at these places when I was straight-identified gave me a bit of a cold shoulder when I came out as bisexual. I found ostracism from both communities, gay and straight.

"I genuinely believe that I am attracted to both men and women. If it is, in fact, a phase, and if I am in the process of discovery, then let me go through it at my own pace. It's just mind-boggling to me how much grief I get from both sides of the sexual fence to decide."

After establishing himself as an out and proud bisexual onstage, Dane smoothly segues to other topics, including a good deal of political observation. "I want to take political comedy back from all the effete intellectuals who have stereotyped it as a smug thing," he comments. "If I can make a factory-worker-, shot-and-a-beer-type guy laugh with me while I'm talking about being a big ol' queer—to me, *that* is an accomplishment!"

And Dane is pleased that his accomplishments are also being recognized by his colleagues. "The best compliment I could have received was from Suzanne Westenhoefer, who said that I was like a bisexual Dennis Miller," he says. "But the way I like to think is, Dennis Miller is like a straight Michael Dane!"

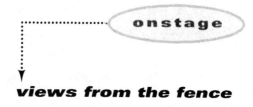

views from the fence

I suppose like most people I really started questioning my sexual orientation when those Soloflex ads started appearing on TV. I don't care what you normally sleep with, these men are *gorgeous!*

Every time I do that joke in comedy clubs, there's always some straight guy who starts laughing and then catches himself—like, "Oops, I've revealed too much!"

Being openly bisexual onstage really screws with homophobes' minds. They're like, "Hey, you're one of them . . . and one of us . . . and one of them . . . I'm so confused!"

When I'm on the road, it's always a little awkward asking people where the queer bar in town is. Actually, it's awkward for the straight guys that I ask. It seems that straight guys think that *knowing* where a gay bar is somehow magically turns them gay, like they'll get fairy dust on them. So if I'm in a small town and want to know where to meet gay men, I usually ask where the Catholic church is.

People don't know how to react when I tell them I'm bisexual. They think I go to clubs and hit on couples: "You both look hot. What do you say the three of us go find someplace quiet?"

People have this attitude that my preference changes day to day, based on my mood. Like I look at the calendar and think, "Damn, it's Tuesday, I'm supposed to sleep with guys today. Where are my pearls?" Or, "I think this weekend I'll pick up a chick. I better find out who won the Bears game."

People think being bi is some sort of dating smorgasbord. It really just means I can go into *any* bar and go home alone.

The word "bisexual," of course, is from an ancient Greek word, meaning "one who pisses off *everyone.*"

I don't even consider myself bisexual. Frankly, I just think of myself as a "people person."

All I'm trying to say is, there's an office in my pants, and I'm an equal-opportunity employer.

A lot of straight and gay friends are in my face, saying, "Why don't you make up your mind? Just choose!" Well, actually, I thought it was like intramural sports, and I was waiting for one of the teams to choose *me.*"

I kept telling myself, "I'm not queer. It's just that all the men that I fall for are."

I don't like labels. I figure if you must put a handle on me (to carry me home more easily), just call me Donny and Marie, because I'm a little bit country *and* I'm a little bit rock 'n' roll.

Labels can also be misleading. I saw a news report about a lesbian protest march, and the reporter said, "Coming up next, a lesbian demonstration." My first thought was, "Cool. I always wondered how those things work."

I did some research on how other cultures treat bisexuals, and I found out that my Native American name would be Dances with Anyone.

Growing up, I remember trying to get all the neighborhood kids to play cowboys and florists.

I suppose my parents had some influence—they did send me off to Donna Summer Camp.

I'm very political. When Clinton was going to reinstate the gay sailor, I thought he should also bring back the construction worker and the Indian chief, because I loved the Village People!

The first queer gig I did was at a gay country-western bar. And to think that some gay people think I'm confused!! Oh sure, country music has always been progressive, right?! Songs like "I'm Gonna Shoot Everyone Who Don't Think Like Me." A gay country bar! It's a little odd to hear someone yell, "You go, Bubba!"

I was in my first pride parade, on the bisexual float. You might have seen it—a lavishly decorated fence on wheels.

The religious right (like that's not an oxymoron!) doesn't even make sense. A group of born-again Christians was at one of our parades (I swear, they show up at more of our events than we do!) and they started chanting, "Get on your knees and repent!" Hey, guys, didn't getting on our knees lead to a lot of our "sins"?!

I'm not always as courageous as I'd like to be. For instance, I'm only out to other people's parents. I'll be in some strange living room, and they'll be looking at me like, "Why are you telling us this?"

Women I date always whine, "Why are all the good men queer?" And I explain to them that they're not—just all the *attractive* ones.

This idea of outing historical figures is getting a little carried away, but it is kind of fun to imagine biblical characters as gay. Picture Moses saying, "Let my people go, girl!"

As a bisexual who's out and proud, I hate that phrase you see in personal ads, "bi-curious." Face it, once you've decided to *advertise*, you' re not just *curious.*

The best thing about being an openly bisexual comic? I can tell the audiences that if they have a problem with it . . . well, they can *all* blow me!

steve
moore

With a wealth of experience as a stand-up comic, Steve Moore came to a conclusion: "Comedy has become generic; everything has been talked about." When Moore started his career in 1980, he says, "Everyone was different in their own way: there was one Jay Leno, there was one Robin Williams, there was one Elayne Boosler. Then we started getting all these comics with a generic brand of comedy."

In 1993, Moore thought to himself, "What have I got to lose by going up there and saying, 'I'm HIV-positive!'? No one's doing that." No one, that is, until Steve Moore. "I'm gay, I'm HIV-positive, and I'm talking about it," he now proudly declares. "I'm doing something that no one had ever done—which is hard to do these days."

For years, in his act, Moore joked about dating girls. "I played it like a little guy who never gets laid," he says, adding with a sudden laugh, "which, actually, was true!"

Some of Moore's colleagues warned that his candor could destroy his career. But, he points out, "Roseanne knows I'm HIV-positive, and she hired me." Moore appeared on Roseanne's HBO special and he's also performed as audience warm-up prior to the tapings of her ABC series. Additionally, comedienne Margaret Cho personally asked Moore to perform the audience warm-up for her 1994–95 series, *All-American Girl,* after she saw him the previous year on Comedy Central's *Out There.*

Moore enjoyed a flood of attention immediately following his *Out There* appearance. Featured on *Entertainment Tonight,* he joked, "Imagine my parents when I had to explain to them that we're Haitian!"

On Fox's *The Mo Show,* he quipped, "People are always saying, 'I can't believe you've been exposed to the AIDS virus. You've never looked better.' I figure, hell, pretty soon I'll be drop-dead gorgeous!"

Moore also appeared on *A&E's An Evening at the Improv.* "It couldn't have been a straighter crowd—a busload of middle-aged businessmen in suits," he recalls "I was nervous that I'd get out there and do my jokes—'A funny thing about AIDS . . . !' —and they'd call the police and put me in a straightjacket!" Fortunately, he reports, the audience was extremely receptive. But that's not always the case. Moore says he occasionally encounters an insensitive heckler. "If I'm going to take the chance and do this kind of material, then I've got to expect that," he says. Nobody said that trying to make a living by exploring the funny side of HIV and AIDS was going to be easy, but, Moore says, "I really feel in my heart that this is what I'm supposed to be doing."

What advice does he offer to someone who is HIV-positive? "Let yourself freak out about it and realize it's big and it could be fatal. Definitely go through those emotions and get your fear out," he says. "But just because you're HIV-positive, your life isn't over. Deal with it, then get on with your life."

you folks are killing me!

The other day I went to the video store and rented *Longtime Companion, And the Band Played On, Philadelphia,* and *An Early Frost.* The clerk asked me to pay cash in advance. I think that's mean!

Can you imagine the AIDS ward in heaven?! The good news is, I may get to meet Rock Hudson. The bad news is, I may have to listen to Liberace music for the rest of eternity!

And if I find out that Liberace is still claiming he's not gay, I'm gonna personally kill the queen *again!*

People ask me if I'm afraid of death. No. I'm afraid of my doctor's bill.

I took one look at the amount of my last bill and I said to my doctor, "I hope to God this figure is my T-cell count!"

Now that I'm out publicly, talking about my HIV-positive status, I've pretty much ruined my commercial career. What could I possibly sell on TV now? "Hi, I'm Steve Moore, HIV-positive comedian, for Doritos . . . careful of the dip!"

I'm starting to get politically correct. I was at the airport last week and I noticed all these signs that say TERMINAL. I'm trying to get them changed to LIFE-CHALLENGING.

I was at the Course on Miracles' HIV-positive support group, and a guy who was HIV-positive was sharing about how he's a cigarette smoker and he's trying to quit. I asked Marianne Williamson if I could share. "I'm HIV-positive and I'm a cigarette smoker," I said, "but I think of it as *white light* going into my lungs, and I *exhale* all the negativity from my body!" By the end of the meeting, everyone was hitting me up for Camel nonfilters!

It seems like every other day there's a new alleged cure for AIDS that later you find out is unfounded. A couple of years ago it was, "Drink peroxide—it oxidizes the blood and kills the virus." I drank that shit for six months, then I went to the doctor to get tested. My T-cells didn't go up at all, but I was constantly complimented as a Marilyn Monroe look-alike!

I hand out condoms at my shows to all the guys who say they're going to have sex later on. I say, "What size would you like, sir? Small, medium, or *'Oh my God!'*?"

I was performing recently, and a straight guy in the audience was heckling me. Finally, I told him to fuck off! Well, this big bruiser started waving his fist at me and said, "Hey, buddy, I could *kill* you with one blow!" I said, "Hey, buddy, *I could do the same to you!*"

My brother says to my thirteen-year-old niece, Jessica, "You know, your uncle Steve is gay and he's HIV-positive." I'm at home over the holidays, sitting down with Jessica— just the two of us—drinking hot cocoa and talking. I'm trying to find out how much she knows about AIDS and safer sex. So I'm telling her some of my jokes, like, "I keep eating Life Savers . . . hoping that they'll work!" She giggled. Then I said, "I have a bumper sticker on my car that says LOSE WEIGHT NOW—ASK ME HOW." She laughed, and I continued. "I don't want to say that my mom is in denial about my being gay, but since I told her that I'm HIV-positive, she's been telling our family that I'm a hemophiliac and a drug user." She laughed some more and gave me a hug.

After our conversation, I told her how wonderful it was that she still loved me and that she didn't judge me. She looked me right in the eyes and said, "Well, Uncle Steve . . . I think it makes you just that much more special."

Then she said, "You didn't drink out of my cup of hot cocoa, did you?"

barry
steiger

Guess who came to dinner on the Thanksgiving 1994 episode of ABC's top-rated sitcom *Grace Under Fire?* The entire clan of Grace's ex-husband—including Deforest, an openly gay cousin. And guess who played Deforest? Openly gay comic Barry Steiger, the founder and first MC of Gay & Lesbian Comedy Night at the Comedy Store in Los Angeles.

In the episode, Grace, played by the show's star, Brett Butler, cringes as a mob of her in-laws invades her home for the holiday. But she brightens at the appearance of Steiger's character, the only one of her ex-husband's family she likes. The two obviously have a lot in common. "Grace and Deforest use intelligent words, words that her ex-husband's family would not be prone to use," notes Steiger.

Similarly, Steiger and Butler have a lot in common. Both hailing from the South, they met in 1983 when they were living in New York City and working at the same comedy clubs.

"We just connected inherently on so many levels—religiously, intellectually, our verbiage," he says. In fact, Steiger, who was ordained a Southern Baptist minister at the unusually young age of eighteen, performed Butler's wedding ceremony.

"I was fanatically religious, but I've changed," he says. Does he miss the ministry? "God, no!" he shoots back emphatically. "If I was at a party, I'd rather meet an ax murderer than a born-again Christian. At least an ax murderer will *eventually* leave you alone!"

It was also in his teen years that Steiger kicked off his comedy career, but he wasn't out of the closet professionally. For that matter, he wasn't out in his personal life, either. "The possibility of my being gay really never dawned on me," he says. But it became crystal clear to him in the late seventies, when he was headlining at, of all places, the Playboy Club. "I have the most ridiculous photograph of me standing between two bunnies, which was taken just moments before I realized that I'm gay!"

After numerous engagements at Catch a Rising Star in New York and Las Vegas, and TV appearances in the eighties on *The Pat Sajak Show* and *The Late Show with Joan Rivers*, Steiger ushered in the nineties by entertaining on board Carnival Cruise Lines. A musician friend on the cruise informed the comic that his relationship jokes, containing the word "she," rang hollow. Steiger quickly wrote his first gay-related joke:

"I don't know why it never dawned on me that I was gay until I was almost twenty-two. I mean, even at the age of twelve, not only was I the only one in my class who knew who Judy Garland was, but when she died, I missed two weeks of school over it! My mother had to send the teacher a note: 'Please excuse Barry. Judy died.'"

During the hiatus between the first and second seasons of *Grace Under Fire,* Butler took her stand-up act on the road, and she took Steiger along to perform as her opening act. "I have balls for having Barry Steiger open for me," says Butler. "Not because he's gay, but because he's such a tough act to follow!" Steiger performed his gay-related material in the act, and he reports, "They loved it! No problem at all!" So if mainstream audiences accept gay-related material, why are there still so few gay characters on TV? He recalls the brouhaha over an episode of *thirtysomething.* "Two guys together in bed—and they weren't even *doing* anything!" he rails. "The first couple that was allowed to be seen in the same bed was the Munsters—and there were cobwebs separating them! If we ever see a gay couple in bed together in a prime-time series, God knows how many cobwebs would have to be separating them!"

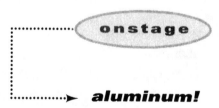

onstage

aluminum!

I saw an article in a gay magazine called "Making It to Forty," and another one about a support group for gay men over forty. I just turned forty. I don't *need* a support group. I have antidepressants, a therapist, and an ever-growing number of twelve-step programs. No, I don't need a support group for men over forty. What I need is a nineteen-year-old wrestling-team captain—*that's* what I *need!*

As it turns out, I've gone from becoming a recovering drug addict to finding out that I'm clinically depressed. I always knew drugs were the answer; apparently, I just wasn't taking the right ones. So now I'm on Desyrel. When I went to pick them up, the pharmacist asked me, "Would you like an easy-to-open bottle?"

"No, I hope to be like Tennessee Williams and choke to death on a childproof pill cap!"

Actually, I think antidepressants should come in a Pez dispenser.

I'm not on Prozac, but I don't buy into the Prozac scare. In the nineties it's Prozac; in the seventies it was Muzak. And I'm certain that far more people have killed people over Muzak than Prozac!

Of course, Desyrel has its drawbacks. When I went to up my dosage, I told the nurse I want to talk to the doctor about some side effects. She said, "What are you experiencing?" I said, "Well, it takes me six times as long to ejaculate." And she said, "*And what's WRONG with THAT?!*"

Of course, people like Pat Robertson would say, "Well, ho-mo-sex-u-als are depressed because they're leading an unnatural lifestyle." You know, it amazes me that when these people talk about traditional family values, they cannot imagine a gay couple in a committed relationship. I was in a totally monotonous, er, monogamous relationship for seven years. And the only difference between my parents' marriage and my relationship with David is that *we were in love!*

And we're friends to this day, unlike my parents, who divorced and were forever trying to blow up each other's cars. If that's traditional family values, I'll take the wacky gay-love thing.

Being gay has never really been that big of a deal for me. Even my mother, who still lives in Louisville, Kentucky, has gotten used to it. I think she's taken it quite well. She can have visitors now, Not every day, and just a few at a time—the rooms are so small where they keep her now.

I didn't even realize I was gay till I was twenty-two. Which is amazing, because I had the straightest, most bigoted, homophobic father any queen could ever hope for. Growing up, he'd say things like, "Well, Barry, what da ya think of them two big boobs?" I assumed he was talking about my uncles.

And I've accepted the fact that I was clearly switched at birth. I say this because I have never had a living thing in common with a single member of my family. It's as though aliens had placed me into this hillbilly family—just for meanness.

By the age of seven—so help me!—I was the only one in my entire family who could pronounce the word "aluminum." Family members would just gather around me and marvel as if I was the Christ child:

"Say it again, Barry!"

"Aluminum."

"Again!!"

"Aluminum!!"'

"He's gonna be another Eeeen-steeen."

And to this day, my mother is forever quoting some old cliché at the singularly worst possible moment. Like, once my cousin was just slightly hurt in a car wreck, and I said, "Well, Mom, she probably wouldn't even have been hurt if she'd been wearing her seat belt." To which my mother instantly replied, "And if a frog had wings, it wouldn't bump its ass when it jumped, would it?"

"No, Mother, I suppose it wouldn't, and thank you for clearing that up."

Or I'd be sitting at the table and I'd choke a little on some food. She'd say, "Maybe that's God's way of saying you're eating too fast."

"Or, Mom, maybe it's God's way of saying you're a shitty cook!"

And we were the absolute last family on the block to get anything new, which was embarrassing. "Oh, Mother, the Stewarts—*they* cook with fire!"

"Well, are *we* the Stewarts? If the Stewarts jump off a roof, does that mean we have to get a roof?!"

Billy Graham has described heaven as a family reunion that never ends. What must hell possibly be like?! Home videos of the same reunion?

People say to me, "Barry, don't you think you'll burn in hell for saying things like that?" No, I do not think I'm going to burn in hell. I think I may suffer some *smoke inhalation*, perhaps.

No, I don't worry about going to hell. I worry about what kind of cologne one wears in hell . . .

Probably Eternity.

jason
stuart

When Jason Stuart competed on TV's *Star Search* in 1987, he sported a vintage tuxedo jacket and zebra-print pants with matching shoes, and the tips of his hair were sprayed fire-engine red. "That was when I didn't want anyone to know I was gay!" he says, fully appreciating the irony. After three wins, he lost to Martin Lawrence, who went on to do *Martin* on Fox. Stuart threw a hissy fit, stamping his zebra-printed feet and stomping off the stage.

In addition to countless comedy club appearances, acting gigs followed, including *Murder, She Wrote* and *Kindergarten Cop.* But it was an appearance on *Geraldo* in the spring of 1993 that changed his life. That was when the comic-actor came out on national TV. "Geraldo was so gracious," Stuart recalls, adding, "and incredibly sexy!" At the end of the show, Rivera even thanked the newly out comic with a smooch!

Stuart, who started performing in 1983, says the possibility never occurred to him that he could be in show business *and* be out of the closet. "I never thought that I would be this out," he says with obvious amazement. "I was thinking that I was going to become a Liberace or a Paul Lynde. And *not* to diss these men—I have a great respect in my heart for them. But, now, that's not what I want to be."

Instead, Stuart wants to be a comic and an actor who's considered for any role, gay or straight. ("What am I going to do, wait for the great hairdresser role? *'He laughs! He cries! He teases your hair!'* ") Career-wise, his biggest dream is "to play a heterosexual in a movie and win an Academy Award, like William Hurt did for playing a homosexual in *Kiss of the Spider Woman.*" In the meantime, he's hot on the comedy club circuit; at many clubs, he was the first openly gay stand-up comic to headline.

While he was headlining at Stanford's Comedy House in Kansas City, Stuart's interview in the *Kansas City Star* attracted not only comedy fans but also a group of fundamentalists who picketed the performance. Says Stuart, "I got to the club and there were people with signs: FAGS MUST DIE! I felt like somebody had thrown a cold bucket of water on my head. It was very scary."

Inside the club, however, Stuart was greeted warmly by an enthusiastic crowd. "I received applause for five minutes before I even spoke, not to mention a standing ovation at the end of the show." Since outing himself, Stuart has likewise tossed his wild costumes out of the closet. "I don't feel the need to be so flamboyant anymore," he says. "I no longer need to push buttons in that way."

my boyfriend's black
(and i'm gonna be in trouble)

I grew up in a crazy family. We were very dysfunctional. What a *surprise!!*

Being gay and Jewish, I would watch all the TV shows in hopes of seeing someone like me. Everyone on TV was so sweet and nice, all widows and widowers raising kids. So I shot my father in the leg so we could be happy too.

My family was so insane. We'd watch *The Partridge Family, The Brady Bunch,* and even *The Cosbys.* We, however, were *the Manson family!*

All the TV families resolved their problems in thirty minutes and everyone was happy pappy. Our problems ended in thirty minutes, too—but ours always involved the police!

My parents are divorced, and my father met a nice gal . . . nice for an eighteen-year-old! They had a wonderful wedding. They served ice cream and cake.

My father bought my stepmother a house in the Hollywood Hills that cost $5 million. My mother got just a little pissed. She stabbed my stepmother. But it's OK. It's a small wound, and she's going to be on *Hard Copy,* so we're real proud.

We had a lot of fights in our family. Now, WASPS know how to have a family fight: they go down to the basement, pull down the shades, talk it over, and everyone's happy pappy. Jews, Blacks, Italians, and Latinos, on the other hand, for a big family fight, we wait for a *holiday!* Your mother runs out on the lawn with a knife! She's wearing a tube top and culottes. She screams, *"Why are you doing this to me?!"* I scream back, *"Because you're wearing a tube top and culottes!! Please take them off!"* And my mother did—right there in front of the neighbors!

As I get older, my brother and I have gotten closer. He always asks me, "What role do you play in a gay relationship? Are you the man or the woman?" I say, "What do you mean what role do I play? I play Patty Duke in *The Miracle Worker!"*

My family had a real problem with my ex-boyfriend, who was black. My mom would always say, "It's not enough that he's not Jewish, he has to be black, too—*and gay?!*

gay and lesbian comics on tv— puh-leeze stand by!

What do Bob Smith and Suzanne Westenhoefer have in common? They're both rising comics, and they're both starring in their own TV specials, airing on cable's Home Box Office.

HBO, the folks who gave a career boost to a number of up-and-coming stand-ups through its *One-Night Stand* specials, is presenting a new series of one-person comedy shows entitled *HBO Comedy Half-Hour*. Smith and Westenhoefer were among the very first comics chosen to participate in the coveted showcase, certain to attract major exposure.

Interestingly, they have something else in common: Bob Smith and Suzanne Westenhoefer are both openly gay.

—Ed Karvoski Jr., *The Guide* magazine, July 1994

bob
smith

Tall, dark, and hilarious, Bob Smith has gone where no other gay comic has gone before. In addition to an HBO special and rap sessions with Howard Stern and Tom Snyder, Smith landed perhaps the most coveted gig for any stand-up—a spot on *The Tonight Show.*

With all this exposure, he felt it was time to phone home. "I said, 'Mom, with HBO and *The Tonight Show,* now everyone's gonna know I'm gay. Are you and Dad OK with that?' And she said, 'Well, your father and I talked about it, and we figured there's a lot of people named Bob Smith. Who's gonna know?' "

Smith sharpened his talk show skills during a half dozen guest spots on Howard Stern's nationally syndicated radio program. People warned him not to do the shock jock's show. "He'll attack you," they cautioned.

Smith dismissed the warnings. "I don't like this idea that I—

or any gay man or lesbian—should be *afraid* of some situation," he states pointedly. "Obviously, there's common sense; you shouldn't put yourself in a self-defeating situation. But we're not victims. We should be able to confront people."

On the night Smith ended up on the *Tonight Show* couch, he says, "They asked me if I wanted to be announced as a gay comedian, and I didn't. The term 'gay comic' doesn't bother me, but in an intro I'd rather not. You don't hear other comics introduced as a 'black comic' or a 'Jewish comic.'" Furthermore, he notes, "Part of the fun of my act is for *me* to tell people I'm gay."

Right after his appearance, with his lover at his side, Smith crossed the street from *The Tonight Show* set at NBC Studios in Burbank to be a guest on Tom Snyder's call-in show, broadcast live on CNBC.

"As a heterosexual man," Snyder posited on camera, "there are some women that I look at that I'm attracted to, but there are many, many more that I'm *not* attracted to. Is it the same if you're homosexual, that you're not attracted to every guy?"

"Definitely the same," Smith replied dryly. "Ernest Borgnine is not on my list."

The following evening, *HBO Comedy Half-Hour: Bob Smith* debuted to millions of viewers nationwide. Veteran comic-activist Robin Tyler shares her feelings about Smith and his ability to reach a mainstream audience. "You cannot tell who is going to hit," she says, "but Bob has the quality that's needed to sustain in Hollywood. He's extremely likeable. Once you have people laughing, you can change their minds. And Bob does it in such a kind and gentle way, and with such a strong writer's position, and with that sweet, little-boy smile—there's just no way you can hate Bob Smith!"

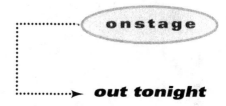

(From Bob Smith's appearance on *The Tonight Show*.)

It wasn't easy telling my parents that I'm gay. I made my carefully worded announcement at Thanksgiving. It was very Norman Rockwell. I said, "Mom, would you please pass the gravy to a homosexual?"

She passed it to my father. A terrible scene followed.

Then my Aunt Lorraine said, "Bob, you're gay. Are you seeing a psychiatrist?"

I said, "No, I'm seeing a lieutenant in the navy."

Parents seem to go through three separate stages of acceptance when they discover that one of their children is gay or lesbian:

At first, they don't talk about it.

Then, they talk about it.

Then, they talk about it on *Oprah*.

We talk about everything in my family now. I remember last year we were talking about gay marriages and my brother Greg said, "Bob, you're gay—what do you think?"

And my mother said, "Greg, that's not nice. Don't remind him."

Oh, yeah, Mom. That had slipped my mind.

* * *

There's been a lot of speculation about what causes homosexuality. So far, no one seems to know. Although, in our family, I was the only one who would drink Strawberry Flavored Nestlé's Quick.

I think you're born gay. Looking back on it, I was a gay kid.

My parents once told me, "Bob, we never suspected that you were gay."

Get real. They once gave me a chemistry set—I used it to make my own line of skin care products.

Now, little boys play with those action figures with the big muscles. It's got to be great for little gay kids.

Imagine—a concerned mother finds her son playing with a Barbie doll, so she runs out and buys him a Masters of the Universe doll.

"Bobby, I want you to play with blond, rippling, muscular he-man—not with Barbie."

"Mommy, that's the best idea you've ever had."

I was definitely a gay kid!

My tree house had a breakfast nook.

My first words were, "Oh, mother, really. . . !"
A gay kid!

I'm a little embarrassed to admit it, but my all-time favorite toy growing up was my sister's Kenner's E-Z Bake Oven. Do you remember this? Of course, the gay guys remember this!

If you don't remember the Kenner's E-Z Bake Oven, it cooked tiny cakes and pizza with the heat from two light bulbs.

This really prepares you for adult life!

The first time I had a dinner party, I tried to cook a roast with a flashlight!

I grew up in Buffalo, New York. Buffalo is very progressive. My high school had a Head Start Program for Homosexuals. It was called Drama Club.

I read that a high school in Seattle tried to ban gay kids from the Student Council. Hey, while they're at it, why don't they ban us from all school activities? Because there'd be no yearbook, definitely no girls athletics, and I'd like to see them try to do *Oklahoma* without us!

I was a nerd in school. One year, I had a Partridge Family lunch box and I recently read that the Partridge Family lunch box is now considered a valuable collectible. That's because very few survived when their owners were beat up.

* * *

The most important fact you should know about me is that my birthday's on December 24. It influenced my entire outlook on life. From years of experience, we people with December birthdays now know what the Three Wise Men said when they delivered their gifts. "These are for both your birthday *and* Christmas."

And according to the Bible, the Three Wise Men didn't even deliver their gifts until January 6. Being wise, they shopped after Christmas.

Last year for my birthday I was given a puppy. It's half poodle and half pit bull. It's not a good attack dog, but it's a vicious gossip.

suzanne
westenhoefer

In 1991—before the term "lipstick lesbian" had been coined; before *Newsweek* proclaimed lesbians chic; and before TV newsmagazines heralded the proliferation of openly lesbian and gay comics—then novice comic Suzanne Westenhoefer appeared on *Sally Jessy Raphael* examining the topic, "Lesbians Who Don't Look Like Lesbians."

How do lesbians feel about being labeled liked that? "I'm not sure how every other lesbian feels," says Westenhoefer, "because, well, you know how lesbians are! We love a little controversy! We *invented* political correctness!"

For herself, she dismisses the lipstick label as "a stupid het thing." But she feels straight people aren't the only ones in need of enlightening. She had also agreed to do the talk show to educate some of her peers, "to let lesbians know that we can look like anything."

Furthermore, the not-necessarily-PC comic says that she's

never had a big problem with labels: "I'm pretty political, but to me, worrying about words seems fairly small in the realm of things. There are bigger things to worry about." In fact, Westenhoefer *welcomes* a particular label. She *wants* to be known —make that *well* known—as a gay comic.

"Some comics say they don't want to be a spokesperson for the gay and lesbian community—that's not me," she says. "I feel very responsible for the gay community—as much as I can. Obviously, I can't represent them all individually. . . . But I can certainly be out there speaking for gay rights—and I intend to!"

Originally from northwestern Pennsylvania ("Yeah, we had gay bars; they were run by the Amish!"), Westenhoefer began her career by performing gay comedy to largely straight audiences at mainstream comedy clubs in New York City. "Telling gay people that it's OK to be gay is not the point," she states, quickly adding, "not that we don't need to hear it *a lot!* But we also need to tell straight people to stop bashing us!"

She's had numerous opportunities to spread that message to a wide audience, including a slew of talk shows, *A&E's An Evening at the Improv, Caroline's Comedy Hour,* and Comedy Central's *Out There.* And—certainly a huge career coup for any comic—she landed her own cable special, *HBO Comedy Half-Hour: Suzanne Westenhoefer,* which debuted in July 1994. She was also recognized with a nomination for Best Comedy Special by the Cable Ace Awards.

But Westenhoefer hasn't gone Hollywood—not yet, anyway. She lives with her lover, a schoolteacher, in Ohio—not where you might expect an up-and-coming performer to reside. "I'm out on the road a lot these days," says the comic. "Right now, I can live pretty much anywhere with an airport."

Of course, Westenhoefer dreams of the day when Hollywood calls and she can hop on a plane, knowing that a juicy film or TV script awaits with her name on it. "I've wanted to be a famous movie star from the time I was old enough to think," she says. But don't mistake this former beauty-pageant contestant (really!) for just another pretty blonde with stars in her big blue eyes; Westenhoefer is paying her dues, crisscrossing the country in her one-woman stage show and earning rave reviews. She's eager to portray lesbian characters, but she's also more than willing to accept a challenge: "I'd win a freakin' Academy Award if I acted straight!"

"you had to make it look like so much fun?"

I've been traveling so much lately. The best thing I did, I went to Mexico on an Olivia cruise—which, if you don't know, is an all-*lesbian* cruise. You know, a whole bunch of lesbians cruise to different places. Oh, no, it's not *cruising*, like the guys do. We're not that cool. We have to use a boat. And it takes a week.

So I'm on this all-lesbian cruise to Mexico, and it was ridiculously hot. It was so ungodly, we were just sweating.

And I thought I could just fight it with powder. I'm walking around and I'm making biscuits! Little ceramic figures are just popping out of my skin!

I took my girlfriend with me . . . and my ex-girlfriend . . . and her ex-girlfriend . . . 'cause that's how lesbians travel.

My girlfriend is one of these really shy, quiet people—good for me! But sometimes she just says the weirdest stuff. We get to Mexico, she steps off the plane, and she goes, "It is hotter than a half-fucked fox in a forest fire." *What?!* But note the alliteration—she's an English teacher! English teachers are tough to date. When we first started dating, I lived in New York and she lived in Ohio, and I would write her all these letters. She'd send them back *corrected!*

And that's hard for me 'cause I have dyslexia and I can't spell. So I write her this letter, and it's all gushy, and at the end I write, "You're my very special *angle.*" She calls me the next day, singing, "Just call me *angle* of the morning . . ." Have you ever done that with words? Like, write a letter to someone and say, "Dear *sweaty* pie . . ."

OK, so back to the lesbian cruise. Just for fun, I took my older sister. You know, my older, *middle-aged, unmarried, doesn't date* older sister, *who played field hockey for six years?* Just a hunch. And she had a *fabulous* time. Well, now she realizes that she's a lesbian! Yes, my thirty-five-year-old sister is coming out!

My mom's blaming me! "You had to make it look like so much fun? Why don't you just take your oldest sister, too, huh? Take her, too!" . . . Who, by the way, is almost forty, unmarried, doesn't date, and played field hockey for six years. It's like, "Mom, you got yourself three dykes here, OK? You're a walking *Donahue* show!"

* * *

Are there any lesbians out there who use that butch and femme thing? No, I didn't think so. And straight people ask you about it, too, and you've got to make up an answer., And you can't use "top" and "bottom," like guys do. That's clever, but it doesn't work for lesbians . . .

"Hey, Suzanne, are you a top or a bottom?"

"Side. I'm pretty much a side. We're both sides. We're bi-side-ual."

But I was thinking, we could keep this butch and femme thing; in fact anybody can use it. We just need a whole new definition, like, the butch is the one that holds the remote control, and the femme is the one that sits beside her going, "Change it . . . change it . . . change it . . . change it . . . change it . . ."

Speaking of butch and femme, I read this book called *Stone Butch Blues*—which, if you haven't read it, you *should* read it, it's really great. But it generated this conversation afterward about what a "stone butch" is. Apparently, it's a woman who will make love to her partner, but not allow her partner to make love to her. All my friends are going, "Oh, that is so sad; that is so weird; I can't believe it; I don't understand it." And I'm going, "*Cool! I want one of those!*" Hey, 'cause sometimes you're just tired, right? . . .

"Oh, God, honey, whew, that was great . . . Good night."

*   *   *

I smoke cigarettes, all right? It's a nightmare being a smoker. Especially on the West Coast. They're so mean about it. It's a lot easier to be queer there than to be a smoker. And those of you who *were* smokers and quit are actually the meanest people in the world. "I quit, I quit, I used to smoke sixty-five packs a day, and then one day I just put them down and quit. You should just . . ." *Shit, bite me, just bite me, all right?!* I really *want* to quit, but it's tough, and everybody's so damn mean about it.

You know, I was thinking of organizing my own Smokers' Rights March on Washington. I'm serious. Get a bunch of us smokers down there, we'll march from the Capitol, down to the Monument . . . well, OK, we probably wouldn't get that far. But we'd chant: "We're here, we're . . . *cough, cough, cough!*"

Well, they'd know what we meant!

the "out generation" of comics in the nineties

Jesse Helms and Rush Limbaugh, you'd better sit down: Gay comedians are suddenly cropping up everywhere.

—Jess Cagle, *Entertainment Weekly,* December 1993

matina
bevis

With a marked southern accent, Matina Bevis informs her audience that she's originally from L.A. "Lower Alabama," she clarifies.

"Most of people's ideas about us are media generated—TV shows like *The Dukes of Hazzard*," she says indignantly. "I'm not saying that there are not rednecks; I'm not saying that there are not people who thought *Deliverance* was a family movie—there are! But I think *Designing Women* was a lot more about the realities of the South today." In solidarity with the show's opinionated Julia Sugarbaker, Bevis quotes, "In spite of being raised and educated in the deep South, I still pay taxes *and* manage to find my way home at night!"

Bevis went off to college with dreams of becoming a dramatic actress—"the next Colleen Dewhurst. But there's not a tremendous amount of roles for girls who are five feet ten. So, consequently, I was doing a lot of Neil Simon [comedies]; I was always playing somebody's aunt."

Additionally, Bevis was always in a position where she could sharpen her comedic skills: "In college, I majored in theater and minored in bartending. Working behind the bar for so long, I worked up a lot of material, which I would try out on the customers."

She finally tried out her material for a much larger crowd when she entered a talent show at the Southern Women's Festival, outside Atlanta. The audience loved her—and so did the festival's producer, Robin Tyler. "She couldn't believe I'd never done [stand-up] before," says Bevis. "Robin immediately started booking me right and left."

The bookings at women's festivals and other gay venues, says Bevis, "allowed me to open up a lot more." Back when she began performing in and around Birmingham, "it was not easy to be out as a lesbian onstage." Noting the old showbiz axiom "Know your audience," she says, "I needed to go somewhere else to make it."

She chose San Francisco. "I like California pretty much," she reports. "I especially like California when it's *not moving!* The idea of the ground opening up and sucking me in is *not* my idea of a good time! I already dated somebody like that!"

Grounded with several years of experience as a stand-up, in 1996 Bevis relocated to Fort Lauderdale, Florida. "Now I want to conquer the East Coast!" she declares.

dating yourself

I've been in a committed relationship for thirteen years. Not with the same woman—I'm a lesbian! What do you think—that I'm abnormal?!

I truly love my partner, and she is a wonderful woman, except for the fact that I think she might be having early senility. For example, I'll be flying back from a gig and I'll call home, and she'll say bizarre things, like, "I've got dinner ready. Don't eat too much on the plane." Like that's even possible! It's Barbie food! I could eat the dinner of every single person flying in coach and still not be full!

You know how everyone has that one special great love in their life? Well, she's not it. I really think that my last lover was "the one." Funny, smart, beautiful, talented. But, God, what a *bitch!*

OK, it was *me!*

I don't know how many of you have ever dated yourselves, but it has its good and bad points. I found out that I am not a cheap date. I went into serious debt trying to impress myself.

And I found out that I am not an easy date. I had to take myself to dinner and a movie *twice* before I would give it up.

It was so great for a long time, but then we started

fighting with ourselves, and it was hell! I mean, where do you go for space?

It was really rough, but everybody in a relationship goes through it. You know how it is when you first meet somebody and fall in love. Everything that they do is wonderful, and you tell your friends, "*This is it! She is the one! The best thing that ever happened to me! We are buying* furniture *and a dog!*"

And then six months or so down the road, when you shake yourselves out of the sheets, some of the little things that she does that are so darn cute just suddenly aren't. And little by little, it starts to drive you crazy. But you've already gone and told everyone you know how perfect she is, this is *it*, she is the *one*—you have bought *furniture* and a *dog!*

You put up with it, but it builds and builds until you realize that you are slowly going mad—*mad*, I tell you! And realizing the source of all this is the beloved, it occurs to you that it's not you; *she* is the crazy one, and she's *making* you that way, too!

Suddenly, you are actually living the movie *Gaslight*. But now you have the perfect out: the bitch is crazy, and she's driving you crazy, too. So now you can go back to all of your friends and tell them, "I *thought* this was *it* . . . I *thought* she was the one . . . but's she's *crazy!*

Now I have my out, because she's crazy. This excuse works really well the first fourteen or fifteen times. But after that, you can't help wondering, "Is it *me*?"

So there I was driving *myself* crazy, and it finally got to the point where I had had just about enough of *me* and *my* bullshit! I mean, who did I think I was, pulling that on *me*?!

So I did it. I broke up with myself. Oh sure, I cried, I hurt. But all the tears and heartache couldn't bring me back to myself.

And breaking up with yourself is not as easy as you may think. I stalked myself in bars. I would call my house at all hours. It just got worse: I kept driving by my house just to *see* if I was home!

Well, when it gets to that point, there's only one sensible thing to do: go down to your local lezbo bar, set up that big snare trap over by the cigarette machine, and catch a new one. And I'm here to tell you: this time, this is *it!* She is the *one!* We have bought *furniture* and a *dog!*

joan jett
blakk

Who's that stylish and articulate talk-show hostess from Chicago? Well, yes, there's Oprah. But there's also Joan Jett Blakk. There are similarities and differences between the two. "We both really enjoy and care about what we do," says Blakk. "Plus, we have the same sense of style, except I'm more like Oprah on ecstasy—*too much* makeup and *too much* jewelry."

Other differences? Joan Jett Blakk's talk show is presented live onstage, not on television. And underneath the plethora of makeup and jewelry, the hostess is a man named Terrence Smith.

"I look more androgynous when I'm *not* in drag," says Smith, who shows up for the interview wearing a snug T-shirt and jeans over his lean, toned physique, accessorized with a black leather jacket and shaved head. "I think I definitely look like a man when I'm in drag. I don't wear fake tits and I don't tuck.

I'll be wearing a skin-tight gown, but there's a bulge. But *out* of drag, I get mistaken for a woman all the time!"

Smith created the cross-dressing character in Chicago in 1989 to perform at functions for Queer Nation and the Radical Fairies. In 1990, Joan Jett Blakk ran for mayor of the Windy City and tallied a couple of thousand votes. And in 1992, the drag queen attracted international media attention as a presidential candidate. Blakk's platform? "Total anarchy! It's always the opposite of what everyone else is saying."

On health care: "Full health care right away! Because I said so! I'm the president, so there!"

On education: "Switch the education and military budgets! Now!"

On gays in the military: "We don't even *need* a military, much less gays *in* it! If I'm elected president, we'll have Dykes on Bikes protecting this country!" (Don't even get this drag queen started on what she calls Clinton's "Don't ask, don't tell, don't care" policy.)

"I'm gonna just keep running till I win!" pledges the presidential hopeful, whose campaign headquarters has relocated. A self-described separatist—"I imagine one day I'll get over it, but right now I kinda like it"—Smith moved from Chicago to San Francisco in 1993 expressly to surround himself with gay people: "You think you're the biggest fag in the world, then you move to San Francisco and you see even bigger ones! It's great!"

The Joan Jett Blakk Show, presented periodically at Josie's Cabaret & Juice Joint, is a combination variety show and chat session featuring community celebs. The topics discussed are as hot as the daily newspaper headlines—which is exactly where Smith gets most of the material. "I especially like looking for those tiny little articles that most people overlook," he says. "Like the pope getting his finger smashed in the popemobile door! I *live* for stuff like that!"

onstage

definitions of community

Every year around June, around the time of the Gay Pride festivals, you start to hear the word "community" bandied about all over the place. And I may well be one of the last gullible sots who actually *likes* the word.

Now, don't get me wrong, I'm still one of the most cynical and bitter people you'll ever meet. (It keeps me young.) However, as I travel around San Francisco, I really have redefined what "community" means to me.

Definition One: Community is all of the boys I have, am, or will in the future "do it" with. All of them. San Francisco is the least private city I have ever lived in. I fucking swore up and down that I was *not* getting in that pool. Oh no. Not me. But my very first boyfriend since moving to San Francisco turned out to be the ex-boyfriend of someone I work with! I'm so sure! I got in the deep end of said pool and I cannot swim. (Negroes do not swim as a rule, anyway.)

Definition Two: Umbrella manners. Now, where I came from—Chicago—people have rotten umbrella manners. In

Chicago, I saw lots of people place a soaking wet umbrella on the seat next to them on the People's Limousine (public transportation); I saw people open umbrellas as they were leaving a building and knock someone over, or put out an eye, because they hadn't looked before they opened. And worst of all, back in Chicago, no one knows how to walk on the same side of the street with someone else who has an opened umbrella without crashing into that person. None of this is true in San Francisco. Absolutely the *best* umbrella manners anywhere!

Definition Three: A very healthy respect for those of us who are closer to a hundred years old than twenty years old. Old people get around here. Nobody fucks with them. People give up their seats on the People's Limo to a dapper old gentleman or a glamour girl who's eighty-five or so. And, honey, it's good to know that old age is no deterrent whatsoever to wearing lots of makeup and jewelry. Of this I am very, very glad.

Definition Four: Skateboard boys. Yeah, they're part of the community, too, ya know! No matter where I am—inside or outside, upstairs or downstairs—I can hear the clickety-clackety, rhythmic sound of a skateboard blocks away. I always stop in midconversation—or whatever—and cock my ear, or maybe I'll run like hell to the window to get a glimpse of the boy muffin riding by. Never an ugly one. And oh my gawd, if he's *barefoot* . . . child, whew! (I actually acquired a skateboard myself on my recent trip to New York City. I can stand on the damn thing, but fuck if I can get it to move. Anyone want to give me lessons? I got the *look* down already, OK?)

Definition Five: I'm walking down Market Street near Castro and up ahead I *see*—mmm, mmm, mmm—a cute young thang coming my way. Oooh, whee! Let me slow down here so I can get a better look. Yes, he's workin' that "soul patch" under his lip and he's workin' those overalls and he's . . . he's a *girl!* OK?! Baby, the wimmin here put the boys to shame, you hear me? Foxy, foxy, foxy. (And it's great when you're on the People's Limo watching the faces of other passengers—well, a few of them, all right?— as they try to figure out who's a girl becoming a boy or a boy becoming a girl. I love that!) Girlies rule in San Francisco. It is one of my dreams to open a girls-only club with a hot-rod, muscle-car theme. Of course, *I* would never actually go inside, but, child, it sure would be fun to sit outside a club like that, OK?

You know, I could come up with more community definitions, but I think you get the idea. We are chin deep in the community spirit that has everything to do with our day-to-glorious-day existence here. The next time you're pondering community, just go for a walk in San Francisco. If you have a long-term-fuck-buddy type of thing going on, you might want to hold that person's hand. More same-sex couples hold hands in this town than anywhere else on earth. That feeling of being able to do that in the first place, is . . .

COMMUNITY!

mark
davis

"I've been around!" drawls Mark Davis as dramatically as Norma Desmond, following with a manic cackle that's patently his very own. Originally from Washington State, he moved to San Francisco (with various stopovers in between) specifically to perform his no-holds-barred comedy, including his one-man performance piece *Faggot with a Gun*. After five years there, he says, "I loved it so much that I did *everything* there was to do—all the venues that I wanted to play, all the shows that I wanted to do, all the men that I wanted to sleep with!

"The good thing about having lived in San Francisco is that you take it with you wherever you go," says Davis, who relocated to Los Angeles in 1995 to expand his market. "Once you've had the privilege to be completely yourself and experience the freedom to be out-out-out-out-out, that mentality stays with you—even if you're performing at Uncle Buck's Chuckle Hut in Bumfuck, Middle America!"

Touring the country gives Davis the opportunity to observe homos in the heartland. "There are some really cool gay people out there; people who are out of the closet in rural areas are a lot more courageous," he says. "But," he adds, "there are also some gay people out there who are really locked up in their own little prisons. The excuse they'll give is, 'It's my job.' Is it worth any amount of money to be miserable all the time? I don't think so."

Observing the people around him is a habitual reflex for Davis. That knack, coupled with a fertile imagination, is also his greatest asset as an artist. He performs a piece—in his words, "a big observational riff . . . a character tangent"—called "If I Weren't Me, I'd Be . . ." "You know how you see people on the street and you make up a personality for them? It's kind of like that," he explains. "America's so violent that you need to do something to get out of your body," he says, adding, "and I can't do drugs anymore because they make me break out in spots . . . in New York and Chicago!"

At different times, Davis wants to be different people, and he does exactly that through his repertoire of characters. "Lately, I most want to be the L.A. dude," says the transplanted comic-actor. "You see them on the streets, and they have those Jesus Christ heroin-junkie washboard abs, you know? And they look really cool and they're accepted by everybody. I look at my life, and I look at their lives, and I think, 'They've got it easy, man!' "

Making it as a performer in Hollywood is definitely not easy, especially for an openly gay actor. "I not only *look* like a gay man, I look like a gay man who's *actually having gay sex,*" says Davis. "That really bothers some people. . . . I really don't *mean* to break the rules everywhere," Davis insists. With a sigh, he adds, "But I tend to."

peter eisenhower westchester III

(One of Mark Davis's many characters, Peter Eisenhower West-chester III, an aging queen, puffs on a cigarette.)

I used to be a fairly well known Hollywood makeup artist. Now I work at the cosmetic counter at Macy's. They didn't want to hire me at first. They thought I was too old or too nelly—as if anyone could be. But I walked right up to that overpainted harlot of a manager and I said to her, I said, "Listen, missy. I was the first makeup man in Hollywood to do under-eye cover on Lana Turner after the Johnny Stompanato incident!" It's true, and it wasn't pretty.

Well, she hired me the next day. Anyway, my first day at the Macy's makeup counter, this woman walked up to me, and she was so ugly . . . I said she was *sooo* ugly . . . *(Audience generally responds, "How ugly was she?")* She was so ugly she asked me what she should use for foundation. And I said, "Spackle . . . and a paintbrush for mascara . . . and an airbrush for lipstick."

And I looked again, and it was *Joan Collins!!!*

I love a good Hollywood story. Oh, and I love *West* Hollywood. It's the only place in America where you can wear two opposing shades of fuchsia in a pantsuit and not get into trouble.

Wasn't always that way, though. Back in the fifties, when Miss Joseph McCarthy and Princess J. Edgar Hoover were queens of everything, everybody equated homosexuality with communism. Now, why anybody would equate homosexuality with communism, I don't know. I don't know ten gay men that can get along in a hair salon, let alone some hippy-dippy commune! I can see it now: "Bitch, what did you do with my hot rollers?!"

The sixties weren't much better, though. Everybody was picketing for peace and love and drugs, but they'd kill any faggot that walked down the street. I was at the Chicago Democratic Convention in 1968, and we did the same work that everybody else did and ran from the riots. That night there was a dance, and I was dancing with my friends, and they told me I had to leave. That was those straight white boys' idea of civil rights. They wanted the women to make the coffee, and they wanted *us* to do the decorating—but they didn't want to hear our voices. No, it's true, and it's not pretty.

Then the seventies came and—disco! We started to dress again. And I met Stuart and we fell in love. We really did. But then I started to go through a change, and I didn't want to have sex so much anymore. And I didn't mind if Stuart fooled around. In fact, I encouraged it. But you gotta understand: then, we didn't know what was out there.

So the eighties came. And Stuart got AIDS.

I remember him looking up at me on his deathbed, saying, "Who knew?!" Now, he was never a very demonstrative person, but before he died, he told me he loved me.

Now, it's the nineties, and life's a whole new ball game. I've got my *(he coughs from his cigarette)* my health. Well, more or less.

You know who I love these days? Those little ACT-UP kids, with their combat boots and leather jackets. *We* wore clogs and sweaters to let people know who we were.

But one thing about the nineties—everybody's worried about their goddamn mortality. But you know what? If Missy upstairs has got your number, she's got your number, and there's not a whole lot you can do about it.

Now, I'm not saying be stupid or unsafe. But for godsake, enjoy your turn!

I don't worry about death. I figure there's a heaven for old queens where angels have sequins on their wings and God's a sister.

And in the last analysis, you can get really angry and bitter about your life, or you can just get really interesting.

And if you haven't heard a word I've said so far, at least listen to me when I say this: attitude without substance is just plain bitterness.

monica grant

You often hear that in order for performers to succeed, they must find their specific niche. But you don't hear that sentiment from Monica Grant. Resisting classification, she says, "My niche is to be someone who does more than one thing." She's a songwriter, a singer, a musician, and a stand-up comic. Plus, she's studying acting and performing in stage plays. "I think that every performer is multitalented; it depends on how they want to express or explore that," she says.

Grant moved from North Carolina to northern California in 1983 and began performing her music. Prior to the move, she says, "I didn't know there was such a thing as women's music. I had no idea." Performing regularly at women's coffeehouses and other venues, she quickly garnered raves. "Grant, who writes all her own material, is considered one of the hottest tickets on the women's concert circuit today," declared the *Woodstock Times.*

"Possessing a ringing alto voice, Grant is a gifted tunesmith," said the *East Bay Express.*

But it was when she added comedy to her act that she felt complete. "I'm not happy doing just the music, and I'm not happy doing just the comedy," she says. "I'm the happiest when I get to do a combination. For me, it's really the whole package."

And Grant is thrilled that other women also are broadening their entertainment interests. "Comedy is getting a bigger and bigger presence in women's culture, lesbian culture, which I think is a real positive thing. For a while, most women's festivals were a little leery of comedy," says the entertainer, who routinely makes the rounds to most of the festivals throughout the country. "But now women are more willing to laugh; they're getting over themselves these days. I think some dykes take themselves too seriously, and it's really nice to see them lightening up.

"Of course, *I'm* into working on myself and processing and all that, but there's a place for that and a place for having fun," says Grant, known for tunes that take a playful look at self-awareness, such as "Codependency Polka." (Strapping on her accordion for the ditty, she admits that the leather straps are her favorite part!)

"To me, mainstream comedy as a whole tends to be less conscious than gay comedy," Grant comments. "The things that make me laugh when I hear gay and lesbian comics are things that some other comics are not even conscious enough to be able to joke about. The comedy I like is more than just laughing at people; it's recognizing things in human nature."

onstage

my kind of woman

When I was growing up, my mother always told me, "Monica, find someone like your father. Marry someone like your father." Well, I knew I was a dyke, but to this day I'm so set on pleasing my mother that I now find myself attracted to women that are balding and have a beer belly. Sometimes it's a problem.

* * *

I get very confused about what dating is. I mean, it's just going out casually and doing things with someone. But if you start sleeping with them and seeing them more often, then is that still dating? Or is that a relationship? Or is it all really the same thing? My only comfort is that no one else seems to really know either.

The other thing about dating lesbians is that they don't stay single for very long. It's like there's this lesbian mating season between relationships. It's about a month long and that's when you gotta nab them, because in a couple of weeks, they're gonna be in another relationship. I just think it would be helpful if we could formalize this mating season—make it, say, a few times a year—so that we would all know when it was coming and could plan accordingly.

* * *

When I reflect on my life and the women I seem to find myself attracted to, I can only marvel. I like unstable women. Sure, you can refer these unstable people to competent therapists, but I prefer to have long-term relationships with these people.

"Monica, I'd like you to meet someone. She's a manic depressive, has a weak grasp on reality, and enjoys water skiing." This is my kind of woman!

codependency polka

You've heard about the Dance of Anger
And the Dance of Intimacy,
But do you know about the dance
That's gaining popularity?
Anyone can do it—I've done it my whole life.
Why it goes back for generations.
It's a hit! It's a smash!
Oh, I wouldn't joke ya,
It's the Codependency Polka!

You push and pull, and spin 'round and 'round,
Swing your partner with your moods
With lots of ups and downs.
Sometimes this polka is tiring to do,
'Cause while you're doing your steps
You have to do hers, too.

The biggest rule is never leave
Even if she steps on your toes.
You do this dance with lots of partners
Because it isn't nice to say "No."
And if I polka perfectly maybe everyone will like me.
Oh, everybody's got a tendency
To do the Polka of Codependency.

I used to have a life,
But now my life is YOU.
And this polka is becoming the only thing we do.
I'd tell you how I'm feeling,
But that might make you mad,
And only happy people polka,
So let's just dance.

robin
greenspan

Born and raised in Southern California, Robin Greenspan con-
cedes she was a Valley Girl long before the genre was immortal-
ized in song. "Except," she wants you to know, "I never got
into malls."

She did, however, get into her father's stash of adult magazines. "I liked my dad's dirty magazines that were hidden in his
closet, which I wasn't suppose to find," she reveals. "But I kept
finding them. I kept finding them *over* and *over* and *over!*" But,
she says, "I didn't know what all that meant; I didn't have a
name for it."

And throughout her school years, Greenspan had crushes on
her Valley Girlfriends. "I've run into some of them as adults,
and they're lesbians," she says. "Looking back, I'm like, 'Her
hair *was* really short, and those girls *were* really, really close!' "

In college, with her sexual identity on hold, Greenspan began to discover her comic identity. Greenspan came out at age twenty-three and began performing as a solo comic just a few years later. As a performer, she says, "I've never tried to hide that I'm gay, but the main focus of my act isn't about being gay. It's a part of my life, just as much as being a woman, being a Democrat, or whatever."

She likes to "just sneak it in," she says, "especially with a straight crowd." For example, Greenspan tells her audience that her Neighborhood Watch Group is a joke: "My neighbors watch my home, but not when I want them to. A guy could be climbing over my backyard fence with a CD player and two speakers strapped to his head in broad daylight, and nobody would say anything. But the *one time* I want to French kiss the Federal Express gal on my own front lawn, they're out with camcorders!"

When the comic delivers that joke to a straight audience, she says, "They're like, 'Did she say *gal?*' " But after the initial jolt, she has them where she wants them. "Straight people might not get jokes about a Gay Pride parade, but they'll understand wanting to French kiss someone they find attractive," she says. "Then, they can relate with me."

Long before Greenspan came out, she says, "I remember watching TV and seeing a report about the Gay Pride parade, and seeing only the Dykes on Bikes and the people in leather and the drag queens, and I'm thinking, 'Well, I guess that's not me.' " She still resents the narrow picture the mainstream media present in its coverage of such events. "Our community as a whole is so diverse, and I'm happy that that's represented within our comedy community, too," says the comic, who made an impressive TV debut on Comedy Central's *Out There in Hollywood,* which first aired in October 1995.

Greenspan wants people—gay and straight—to see the many faces that make up the lesbian and gay community. And that includes a lesbian Valley Girl!

onstage

kung pao and coming out

I don't do a lot of gay jokes. Frankly, I don't see the humor in it. Like the whole gays-in-the-military thing—not funny. And I know from firsthand experience; I was kicked out of the army for being gay, and it was devastating! They took away everything! My uniform! My dignity! My bucket! My bell! . . .

OK, it was the *Salvation Army.* But that doesn't make it funny!

Did you hear about that woman who got $3 million for spilling hot coffee on her crotch at McDonalds? Three million dollars!! I wish someone had given me that option before I wasted all that time in college! If they had just laid it all out for me, "OK, you can spend four to five years at a local university, graduate, and earn maybe $30,000 a year, working every single day for the rest of your life. *Or . . .* scalding java in your cooch—three million!"

I'd be like, "Could that be decaf? I get irritable."

Why even bother working? They say most people hate their jobs. I have this friend who hates her job. She's a *doctor!* But she hates her job. She refuses to watch that television show *E.R.;* she says, "Robin, I'm off work, I don't want to be reminded of work." I'm like, "OK. But, Mary . . . you're a *lesbian gynecologist!!"*

That has to be the ultimate excuse for getting out of sex: "Honey, not tonight. I had a long day at work. I saw a lot of patients. I can't even *look* at another vagina, OK? I've got vagina up to *here,* all right? *I'm all vagina'd out!!"*

＊　＊　＊

I came out to my mom in the parking lot of the New China Mandarin Buffet on the corner of Saticoy and Balboa. Are you familiar with it? It's an excellent place to come out if you happen to be in Van Nuys. Plus, they have great kung pao.

So we have lunch and then I walk my mom to her car. All I said was, "Mom, I've got something to tell you." That's all I said. Right away she doubles over, knees in the gravel. I had to help her back to her feet. I said, "Mom, it's all right. I love you, and I'm gay."

OK, I really wanted to say, "I'm a lesbian," but I thought

that's just *way* too many syllables to be pummeling at the poor woman in her condition: "*Lez!* . . . *bee!* . . . *an!*"

I just said, "Gay." I'm in, I'm out of there—nobody's badly hurt.

So, clutching her chest, my mom says to me—and I'm not even kidding!—she says, "Oh, my God! I feel like when Kennedy was killed!"

I'm like, "Really, Mom? Bobby or Jack?"

So I'm in therapy now. I used to be in denial, which was, well, a lot cheaper.

I always encourage people to get into therapy, because it's good for you and it's not hard. It's like a really easy game show, where the answer to every single question is "My mom."

I'm working on self-esteem issues with my therapist. So she gives me this exercise where I'm suppose to stand in front of a mirror and repeat over and over again, "I love myself. I love myself. I love myself." And she says it's best if I do it totally naked. Which made me a little uncomfortable because, apparently, she wanted me to wait until I got *home.*

So now I'm seeing a *new* therapist. The very first day I go to see him, he sits me down and says, "Now, before we get started, I want you to know that I work on a fifty-minute hour." At first I thought, "What? I'm coming to *him* for help?!" But then I figured it out. They need that extra ten minutes to get on the phone and just dish you to all their friends: "Oh, my God, she's *crazy!* She's *insane!* Oh, I gotta go. I got another freak daddy at the door."

Fifty-minute hour! But I didn't say anything. At the end of the session, I just handed him a check. And he says, "Excuse me, but this is only for *half.*" And I say, "Oh, I'm sorry, I should have told you earlier. I pay with a fifty-cent dollar . . . so it all works out evenly!"

e. l.
greggory

"Being a young gay person and not having role models—I think that gives you a bit of a twisted perspective," says E. L. Greggory. "So I think we, as gay people, are more likely to be a little more comically oriented, because we *have* to be. As outsiders, we have a need to make things funny."

That innate reflex to make things funny may have expedited her apprenticeship in the comedy ranks. When Greggory first auditioned at the Comedy Store in Los Angeles, she instantly impressed the club's owner; the comic skipped the customary runs of the showcase ladder and was immediately offered paid bookings.

Onstage, Greggory's delivery is as crisp and sharp as her joke writing. Additionally, she projects the image of a confident, strong woman—contrary to the image she was exposed to as a youngster. "I didn't fit the 1950s–60s stereotype of females that you saw on TV. And I felt out of place in my small town," says the Wisconsin native. "That's part of what drove me to realize that I wasn't like a lot of other people—not being gay per se, but simply being aware of not having strong female role models, gay or not."

While television offered no role models for her to emulate, Greggory, a resourceful and perceptive child, did manage to find a heroine. "As a kid, I used to ride the buses from Oshkosh, Wisconsin, to my hometown, and I was quite taken by this woman whom I'd always see. She looked like an artist, she dressed differently than other people, and she carried herself differently than other people—especially other women. I didn't want to date her or marry her or go to bed with her; I wanted to *be* like her—a strong, confident woman."

That woman, says Greggory, "was probably my biggest role model—someone I saw on a bus! And, as it turned out, today I think I *am* that woman."

Greggory believes that the presence of openly gay and lesbian performers will provide role models for future generations. "We've got to get out there in the mainstream. That's where the real challenge is," she says. "When I perform for a straight crowd, I clearly sell myself as a gay person, not as a *covert* gay person, *not* as a neutered household pet." As for an equitable representation of openly gay and lesbian characters on TV? Assuredly, Greggory predicts, "The day is coming when we're going to see it."

growing up catholic and other perversions of nature

I'm angry at the Catholic church, because it says that women can't be priests. Right. Like my big dream is to run around in a long black dress and fuck altar boys. But I think I should have the choice.

The pope agrees that women cannot be priests, and this is his reason: because there were no women priests when Jesus lived. And that's true. But there was also no pope. Does that stop him?

The Catholic church looks at the fact that Jesus never married and had an all-male ministry, and it says that this means Jesus didn't want women priests. But is that what it means? I don't think so. I think it means Jesus was gay. Think about it. He never got married, never had a girlfriend, never even dated. He hung out with twelve other guys his entire adult life. The only woman in his adult life was Mary Magdalene—and we can all agree she was a fag hag.

The Catholic church does not like homosexuals. Well, it doesn't like *male* homosexuals. Because I've read the Good Book (I'm talking about the Bible, guys, not *GQ*) and it says that a man shall not lie with a man as he lies with a woman. But it says nothing about women lying together. Nothing at all. Does that mean that God forgot about women? I don't think so. God is God; God doesn't forget. I think God was saying, ''Go for the gusto, girls!''

Or maybe it's that God is just like every other straight man—he likes to watch women do it. So he invented lesbians. Kind of like having his own private Playboy Channel.

Besides, I do not understand why the Catholic church is so opposed to lesbians, because everyone knows lesbians don't have sex. They just move in together and begin to raise cats. Which is ironic if you think about it. There's all those pussies running around the house, and nobody's getting any action.

My mother is very Catholic, and as a result, she's had a difficult time coming to grips with my sexual orientation. When I told my mother I'm gay, the first thing she said to me was, ''Well, if that's what you want to do with your free time, I suppose I can't stop you.'' She thinks it's a hobby. Kind of like swimming. What I'm really afraid of is that at the next Olympics, she'll look for a new event— muff diving. And I'll be going for the gold.

My mother did ask me if I was a practicing lesbian. I had to be honest with her. I told her no, that I've gotten very good at it, and I don't have to practice anymore at all.

I had a hard time telling my parents I'm gay, so I broke the news to them gradually—I told them I wasn't gay, but, the woman I was sleeping with was.

* * *

I don't like Gay Pride parades. I do not understand grown adult men dressed like nuns, marching down the street, screaming they want equal rights. They say, "You won't give us equal rights because we're gay." No, it's because *you're dressed like fucking nuns!* I wouldn't give equal rights to a *straight* man dressed like a nun. I wouldn't give equal rights to *nuns.*

Then there are the Dykes on Bikes. Have you seen these girls? They drive big jackhammers on wheels. They dress in leather and wear these big, black jack boots. They have their hair buzz cut. Every body orifice is pierced with metal. And they protest, "You won't let us be schoolteachers because we're gay." No, it's because *you'd scare the shit out of the kids!* Get a life. Get a wardrobe.

I do not care whether they allow gays in the military or not, because the whole idea of the military strikes me as completely absurd. I do not understand the desire to pick up a gun and go off and shoot strangers when there are so many loved ones I'd like to take a shot at first. I'd have to reload several times to get everyone on my particular hit list of love. Think about it. What sense does it make to go off somewhere, thousands of miles away, to a scorching desert, for example, to kill a lot people who have never done anything to me—when I can sit in the air-conditioned comfort of my own home and take out a few people who really matter?

paul
jacek

At a coffee shop in Studio City, California, Paul Jacek orders a Delicious Hamburger (yes, that's actually what it's called on the menu). Apropos, he requests, "Hold the secret sauce."

Indeed, there have been no secrets between Jacek and his audiences ever since he started performing as a stand-up comic in 1989. "People take one look at me and they know I'm a big ol' fag," says the comic, who often dons kitschy rhinestone accessories. "I might as well just trot it out there—and it has always worked."

Several years before the Comedy Store in Los Angeles introduced its Gay & Lesbian Comedy Night, Jacek began performing there, alongside straight comics, for predominantly straight crowds. Jacek says he was the target of homophobia, *not* from the audience or the club owner, but from other comics. "There was a nasty female comic who followed me, and after I did my set, she used to wipe the microphone off," he says. Male comics, too, would taunt him. The club owner suggested to Jacek that he not go to his car alone following the show. "I kept wondering, 'Am I willing to die for this?' I didn't dwell in fear, but I was real careful. Thank God things have changed a great deal."

Now, he says, it's common for people to approach him after a show to offer gratitude. But while advances have been made, his openness is still not always received warmly. As a contestant in a stand-up comedy competition, Jacek performed all over his home state of Colorado, including a performance at the Air Force Academy in Colorado Springs. Recalls Jacek: "A guy in the front row yelled, *'Die of AIDS, fag!'* And I said, 'My lover, Jim, just did a few months ago—feel better?' "

At the time of Jim's death, in 1994, the two had been together for ten years. "He was always my most staunch supporter and biggest fan," Jacek says of his late lover. "I lost about a dozen friends around the same time," he says. "Now, in my mind, I put them all at a table in the back of the room wherever I perform. That way I never have a bad set, because I'm performing for a group of people that just love me and think that I'm the funniest person they've ever seen."

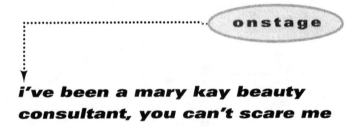

i've been a mary kay beauty consultant, you can't scare me

Hello. My name is Elizabeth Taylor . . . and I'm an alcoholic. No, no, no. I don't need to pretend to be anyone else.

God knows, my life in Hollywood is glamorous enough. This morning I woke up, tossed my golden curls against the satin pillows, walked to my window, and opened it— they're French doors, of course. Woodland animals come in to help me dress. No one ever doubts this.

But my life hasn't always been so glamorous. I grew up in Longmont, Colorado. Such an open-minded state, huh?! After I corrected another first-grader and said that Barbie's best friend was Midge, not Skipper, it was twelve *really long years.*

Perhaps you remember me. I was the kid who had the fresh apple for the teacher every day. I was the kid who had the answer to every question ("Pick me, *pleeease,* pick me"). I was the only boy in the entire school who had a Bobby Sherman lunch box. Yes, I was the class sissy.

When I was in the fifth grade, I went to the library to look for a book about these special feelings I had. I'm at the card catalog. I look up "homosexual." The card says, "See librarian."

Even Santa Claus disappointed me. Christmas morning, I rip open my package . . . it's Sergeant Rock Walkie-Talkies! In my letter, I had specifically asked for a set of Princess phones with light-up dials! I learned at an early age that it wasn't easy being enchanted. Not everyone gets to be enchanted. Only one in ten. Or as I prefer to think, two in twenty—it's less lonely.

Only once did I—the class sissy and model student—do anything wrong in school. I was late coming back from recess. Forty-five minutes late. Fortunately, I had a good excuse. I was tied to the tetherball pole. As my teacher, Mrs. Billings, cut me down, she asked me a stupid question. And later on, my eighth-grade teacher, Mr. Herring, would ask the *same* stupid question as he pulled me out of a locker I'd been stuffed into. "Why do you *let* them do this to you?"

Even my own mother said to me, "We had two sons . . . then we had you."

I tried to fit in. In high school, when my two perfect older brothers, Tim and Terry, played football, I did what I could. I was a cheerleader. Later on, when they went into the navy, I did what I could. I became a tour guide for the *Queen Mary*. Have you been to the *Queen Mary*? It's a quite popular tourist attraction in Long Beach, California. Next to it used to be Howard Hughes's airplane, the *Spruce Goose*. Being a tour guide there was OK, but then one day I realized I was on a ship that didn't move, next to an airplane that didn't fly . . . and I wondered why my life wasn't going anywhere.

I was in a relationship for ten years with a wonderful man named Jim. He was a Roman Catholic Quaker. At least he was quiet about his guilt.

And then he died. People get weird about death. All I really know is that it has something to do with ham. "Jim is dead, here's a ham."

I got three honey-baked!

And if it's cancer, you get scalloped potatoes.

I'm single again, so I'm dating. So, of course, I've started working out at the gym. So far, I have a *one*-cep.

And I don't care what your persuasion is, dating is weird! I was on a blind date recently. The guy said to me, "Hey, Paully, I'm going to take you to a place you've never been before." I didn't know what that meant either. But I've been a Mary Kay beauty consultant, you can't scare me.

So we end up at the Richard Nixon Library in Yorba Linda, California. Leave it to me—someone who makes being a stereotype a full-time job—to find a Republican fag! At least I was able to appreciate the architecture . . . and laugh at Pat's bad taste in inaugural gowns.

We walked outside to the Tricia Nixon Cox Rose Garden. I just love saying that—the Tricia Nixon *Cox* Rose Garden. And my date said, "Paully, I think we should just be friends."

I said, "With whom?"

I recently performed at the Air Force Academy in Colorado Springs, Colorado. Can you imagine? Five hundred strapping cadets . . . and me! Performing there that night, I learned the difference between quiet and silence.

After the show, this redneck came up to me and said, "What do you want me to call you? Queer? Fag? Homo?"

And I said, "You can call me . . . Paul Jacek."

sabrina
matthews

What advice does Sabrina Matthews offer to aspiring stand-up comics? "Get onstage as much as you can," she states emphatically. Matthews first got onstage at a talent show while working as a counselor at a summer camp in Connecticut. At her impromptu debut, she joked about her mother's practice of unplugging the microwave at night out of concern for the safety of her cats. "As if one of them is going to climb in there, punch in a cook cycle, then get the other cat to hit the 'start' button as part of a suicide pact they've arranged beforehand."

A few months later, while coaching the women's rugby team at Yale University, Matthews attended an evening of gay cabaret presented on campus ("It was called 'Cabar-gay,' which I thought was rather imaginative") and she was once again drawn to the stage. "The whole show consisted of men singing, men taking their clothes off, or men singing *and* taking their clothes off," she recalls. "I walked up to the woman who was emceeing and said, 'Put me onstage.' She said, 'What are you going to do?' I said, 'I have no idea, but I promise not to sing or take my clothes off.' "

Matthews got onstage and told the crowd that she was a victim of "a drive-by shouting." A couple of guys in a Ford Pinto—"or some fine piece of automotive workmanship"— pulled up to her. One of the guys, she continued, "rolls down his window a chicken-shit four inches, looks at me, and says, 'You're a dyke!' I said, 'Well, you're an asshole.' I guess he thought we were going to fling insults back and forth, but for me it was a simple exchange of factual information."

Drawn to comedy stages ever since, Matthews has honed her storytelling style of humor at both mainstream clubs and gay venues since 1991. "I tend to approach comedy like a lot of the young, straight guys that I work with, and I think that has a lot to do with the fact that I was in the right place at the right time; I was able to walk into a comedy club as a comic—not as a woman comic and not as a lesbian comic, but as a comic." She credits a number of performers, particularly Scott Capurro, for paving the way for openly gay and lesbian comics to get booked at mainstream clubs in San Francisco. To become a regular on the comedy club circuit, she notes, "You have to work your way up through the ranks—and they're not easy ranks for *any* comic."

Matthews's advice for openly lesbian or gay comics in particular? "There's plenty of people in the world who are making fun of gays and lesbians. Don't be one of them."

happy national coming out day!

I like to walk around the Castro in San Francisco and watch the straight people that come visit. You can always pick the homophobic sightseers. They're always in a couple. There's a really big guy . . . with a really tiny girlfriend . . . with really big hair. And the man is swinging the woman around, because he doesn't want the lesbians to touch her . . . because she will change.

Sometimes I want to say these guys, "You know, we can't just brush up against your girlfriend in the street and switch her over. It generally takes five to ten minutes over a cup of coffee!"

I always follow these couples—watching the woman dangle her legs in the air, pretending that she's walking—and I wait to hear something ignorant. Whenever I hear someone say something like, "Look at that fag," I'll get right up behind the couple, and very quietly so that only he and she can hear, I'll say:

"How much for the girl?"

This will keep them safe for the rest of their short visit.

* * *

We gay people have National Coming Out Day. I actually have a couple of problems with National Coming Out Day. First of all, I can *never* remember it. October 11 is a totally arbitrary date. If National Coming Out Day was the first Monday in October, and I got a three-day weekend because I'm queer, I could remember it. As it is, I'm always looking at my watch on October 14 and I'm like, "Shit, I forgot to come out *again!*"

But I guess what really bothers me about National Coming Out Day is that Hallmark Cards hasn't gotten on the wagon. Something like:

Dear Mom,
I chose this very special day
To let you know that I am gay.

or

I know I played football and baseball and tag,
But now I play disco 'cause I'm a big fag.

I wrote one for myself, or rather one that I'd choose if I found it at card store. Mine would go:

Roses are red,
Violets are blue,
I'm a lesbian,
And so is Aunt Phyllis.

Actually, if Hallmark wants to use my idea, I'd suggest that card say, "So is Aunt _____," and you could write your aunt's name. And if you didn't have an aunt, you could write your uncle's name. Boy, that would spice some shit up around the dinner table, huh? "I'm a lesbian, and so is Aunt Bob."

"Bob? My brother is a lesbian?! Is that where my brassieres have been going all these years?"

* * *

Someday, I want to go to this town in Michigan called Dyke. Every year, all of the women on their way to the Michigan Womyn's Festival make a pilgrimage to Dyke to have their pictures taken at the Dyke city-limits sign, and they make pyramids in front of the Dyke town hall. Apparently, the citizens of Dyke don't appreciate this yearly pilgrimage. Every year they go out and take down all the signs that would direct people to their town.

To me, that sounds like a lot of trouble. If they don't want us to visit, just change the name of the town. Change it to "Uptight Straight White Guy"—we'll stay away.

* * *

Being a lesbian has apparently become quite fashionable. I have a friend, a gay man, who told me he wants to be a lesbian. He called me up at seven-thirty in the morning after a nasty all-night breakup. He said, "I hate men; I want to be a lesbian." I said, "You mean so you can *dwell* on this relationship for longer than it actually existed?!"

He's obviously recovered, because he got a *penis* tattooed on his arm. Another friend of mine, another dyke, looked at it and said, "Wow, that's so great! You had a *dildo* tattooed on your arm!"

*   *   *

I'm not a radical feminist comic. Of course, for some audiences, that's an oxymoron and for others it's redundant.

I do a lot of traveling as a comic. I've traveled through the Bible Belt. "Belt" is too narrow a word, I think. It should be "Bible Cummerbund." Or maybe "Bible Body Cast."

I was recently in a comedy show in Dayton. When the producers called me up, they said someone recommended me because they needed a "strong lesbian." I thought, "Well, do you want me to tell jokes or *move shit*? 'Cause I'll move shit, but it'll probably cost you more than the jokes. And there might be a dyke in your town who could move that shit a lot cheaper."

Another time, I was performing at a comedy club and when I said I'm a lesbian, a guy in the audience yelled out, "Can I watch?" I said, "Watch me what? Fix my car?"

lynda
montgomery

"It's one thing to tell your parents that you're gay. It's another thing to tell them that you trash them for a living!" laughs Lynda Montgomery, who not only works as a stand-up comic but also teaches a comedy workshop in the Los Angeles area. "People laugh at things they can relate to," she tells her students. "Your family is a good subject for material—everybody has one."

In her act, Montgomery says that her mother was shocked when she first learned that her daughter is a lesbian—but she's gotten used to the idea. In fact, Mom expressed that she "wouldn't mind having a lesbian experience."

"That's the grossest thing I've ever heard in my life!" blurts Montgomery. "It's bad enough thinking of her naked with my father! Someday I'm going to be out dancing, having a good time, and I'll turn and see my mother dancing with Bea Arthur! I'm just not ready for that!"

Neither was she ready to joke about her sexual orientation

her very first time onstage, in 1990. Almost immediately, however, she incorporated gay-related material, which she says improved her act immeasurably. "People are always interested when you reveal something personal about yourself," she now advises her students. "The most important thing you can learn is that your material should be about you."

Montgomery's career goal, she says, "is to qualify for a mortgage as an out lesbian comic." But whether or not her students pursue a career in comedy, she believes they can all benefit from their new skill: "It's great for stress reduction!"

She also recommends that the aspiring performers gain stage experience by performing at fund-raisers and pride festivals. In fact, Montgomery, who grew up in a small town in Canada, gets some of her best material at pride events. "My hometown was so small that I was all alone in the Gay Pride parade. I was grand marshal, I was security, I was Dyke on Bike. By the time I peddled my Schwinn across town, I was too tired to even go to the festival!"

Now the small-town girl is playing for some large, appreciative crowds. A highlight of her career was her performance on the main stage at the 1993 March on Washington, in front of an estimated 1 million people: "I hadn't seen that many queers since the Academy Awards!"

Assessing her grads, she declares, "I've created some stiff competition for myself!" But she's not really worried. Montgomery believes there's room for everybody to shine in the showbiz spotlight. "There are a lot of stars on the Hollywood Walk of Fame," she observes. "Maybe someday we'll see some triangles!"

closet comic

My family are funny people. When I told my father that I'm a lesbian, he delivered a comeback like a pro. "Oh, that's great! It will save me on a wedding!" (My little sister was on her second husband at the time. I'm thankful that homosexuals can't get legally married yet; I'd be right up there with Zsa Zsa Gabor and I'd be paying more alimony than Johnny Carson!)

My parents have been together for forty-five years because they find each other so amusing, and humor makes life easier—plus alcohol and Valium! (I could have left out that part, but most good humor comes from blunt, unfiltered honesty.)

I think of myself lovingly as white trash. More specifically, white *trailer* trash. I was raised in a paneled hallway.

My parents recently made up their will. They let me know that everything was being split equally between myself and my only sister; she was getting the house, but I was getting the wheels and the porch.

With that kind of inheritance, I ask myself, *Why do I even work?!*

My entire family are all hard workers. My mother

holds all the sales records for Avon ladies. Her secret was to follow Jehovah's Witnesses around, so that people would be happy to see her.

It was her compulsive desire to use cheap cosmetics that drove her door-to-door as a dealer.

When I was a kid, she would take me with her as a demo model. My inner child looks like Tammy Faye Bakker! I became the class clown, not because I was funny, but because I wore too much makeup!

As a kid, I lived for show-and-tell; I considered it stage time! I relate to the book *Everything You Ever Needed to Know You Learned in Kindergarten;* I still glow as I remember the laughs I got sticking crayons up my nose!

On my report card, a teacher wrote, "Lynda is like a bright and shiny light that is always on. I just wish she wasn't 'on' in my classroom!" (My mother was a teacher, so I'm sure she empathized and, at the same time, was thankful for the break.)

My childhood inspiration was John Boy Walton. He wanted to be a writer, and he was disciplined enough to turn everything into a teleplay and get himself a series! This, to me, was success. If a hick like John Boy—who was so poor he had to wear the same overalls in every episode —could do it, so could I!

John Boy was my first hero, but his sister Mary Ellen was my first crush. In my fantasies, it was Mary Ellen who wore the overalls in the Walton family! If they brought *The Waltons* back to television now, there would have to be at least one gay kid in the family. John Boy could have a younger brother: Boy George!

The only subject I liked in school was English. Math was my worst. In high school, I could not pass a math test. I couldn't have passed a *drug test* either—there may be a correlation there. It's been proven now that marijuana destroys your memory, so maybe all the pot I *thought* I smoked is actually still hidden in my bedroom. That could explain my limited memory of childhood. According to a therapist who I once dated, lack of childhood memories can be related to either something traumatic, or—worse—a childhood that was so boring that it's better to just forget!

I do remember that my childhood revealed an inability to deal with authority figures. I was kicked out of Brownies, sent home with a note saying that I did not have respect for my elders. This, from a fifty-year-old woman who wanted me to call her Fluffy Owl!

My early problems with authority should have given me a clue that, as a young adult, the military would not be a good career choice for me. But a strong desire to serve my country (as something other than a waitress) and an even stronger desire to *get out of a small town* drove me to the recruiter's office at the tender, not-out-of-the-closet age of seventeen.

Basic training is a closet case's dream come true! Ninety women in close quarters, wearing fatigues and black boots, and not allowed near the men. I blossomed! I could not believe my good fortune! Five years later, my whole life changed when an officer accused me of being a *lesbian!* I would have denied it, but I was laying naked on top of her at the time.

Somehow, everything worked out as it should; my love of show-and-tell came back into my life in the form of stand-up comedy. (And my discomfort with "Don't ask, don't tell" led me to be an out lesbian comic!)

I love being a comic. I think the true test of how much you like what you're doing is to take the "If I won the lottery, would I quit my job?" test. I gave it some serious thought. In all honesty, if I did win the lottery—as much as I love being a stand-up comic—I would *never* say another amusing thing!

marilyn
pittman

It's a common scene to PBS viewers nationwide: the din of telephones ringing, rows of volunteers answering those phones and scribbling pertinent information, and in the center of it all, a local celebrity fervently barking for your buck. But this particular pledge night on KQED in San Francisco is in some ways different from many in other parts of the country. As the lesbian-themed film *Last Call at Maude's* is being broadcast, in December 1994, the hosts rehearse the next live segment.

"Good evening, I'm Marilyn Pittman, comic and broadcaster and big star." She directs a "just kidding" shrug to the stage manager. "How about pledging $120? I know there are a lot of you *guppies* out there, and that's not that big a bite! Use your credit card and s-p-r-e-a-d out the payments.

"C'mon, stand up and be counted among those people who support [KQED's] commitment to celebrate diversity, not abandon it—like the Republicans." Pittman shoots a look to the director and asks, "Can I add that last part?"

No, she can't, she's told. She winces and continues.

"And for you un-gays, I think it's time you supported *our* history, like we've supported *yours.*" The teleprompter comes to a sudden halt. "Can I add *that?*" she begs. "I think it's important." She gets her way. She's cued, and she repeats it live on the air.

For many years Pittman juggled her careers as a broadcaster and a stand-up comic. But since her move from Albuquerque to San Francisco in 1985, she sees the two, together with her passion as an activist, synthesizing.

"In Albuquerque, I was fired for being gay," says Pittman, who worked there as a rock radio DJ. "In San Francisco, I was *hired* for being gay." In 1991, the local chapter of GLAAD (Gay and Lesbian Alliance Against Defamation) lobbied radio station KGO to present a balance to Rush Limbaugh's conservative program. Pittman, who previously worked at the KQED radio station, was brought on as a talk show host. "All of a sudden, I found an avenue for my comic persona on the radio," she says. "I'm part journalist, part comic." And always a totally out lesbian. "I dealt with gay issues on the show a lot," she says. "I found that radio audiences were more intelligent and more sensitive than I thought they'd be."

But there's hardly a timely topic that Pittman hasn't explored in her comic commentaries, which have aired in San Francisco and on other National Public Broadcasting stations. "I'm gay, that's part of me—a *large* part of me because I'm an activist," she says. "But I'm also a middle-class WASP, born in the fifties in the middle of the country, and raised on Spam," adds Pittman, originally from the same hometown in Illinois as Lea DeLaria. "All that is part of my perspective, too."

Oddly enough, Pittman says she learned how to express her perspective humorously by studying her antithesis, Rush Limbaugh! Says Pittman, "I don't want to come off as a strident leftist. I want to come off as a *funny* leftist. Rush Limbaugh has succeeded because he's funny. He's more of an entertainer than he is intelligent." Exaggeratedly, she blurts, *"That we know!"*

i was a teenage lesbian

Yes, I was a teenage lesbian! And while that may sound like a horror movie to some of you, for me I could subtitle that period of my life "Adventures in Paradise," because there was one thing that we gay teenagers could do that our straight friends couldn't. I could say, "Hey, Mom, Michelle's comin' over to spend the night Friday night, OK?"

"OK, honey!"

Johnny couldn't come and sleep over, but Michelle could! I was having sex regularly at the age of sixteen in my parents' house with a *woman!*

It's at this point of my act, when I perform in San Francisco, that you can hear the tourists mumbling to each other: "Oh, Fred, good. Our trip to San Francisco is complete. We saw a les . . . les . . . les . . . a *dyke!*"

Because we are, after all, one of the biggest tourist attractions the city has to offer. It's the bridge, the wharf, the queers.

I think there should be a gay tax just for letting the tourists come into the Castro to look at us. And they *do* look at us! They come in on those red double-decker London tour buses and *look* at us! One day, I'm sitting in front of Josie's Cabaret, having a cup of coffee, and this big red double-decker London tour bus pulls up right there on Sixteenth Street, and all these pairs of eyes are looking at *me!*

I heard a lady say, "Oh, look, I think that's one! She has lesbian haircut number four! That's what it says in the brochure!"

* * *

Good old capitalism! Where there's money to be made, there's always a veneer of tolerance.

I received a mailing from AT&T—you know, the ones who keep calling us.

"Miss Pittman?"

"Yes."

"It's AT&T. We want you back."

"It's a little late, AT&T."

"We didn't know what we had until it was gone."

"Just like all the others!"

So this brochure I received is printed on lavender paper, and it shows a rainbow-colored phone cord and pictures of same-sex couples. Here's a gay male couple, and one of them is saying, "When David's away on business, we like to stay close." Yeah, right! He and David are having phone sex! And the phone company's making money on that, too!

Enclosed with the brochure was this letter:

Dear Marilyn Pittman:

At AT&T we believe it's important for you to feel good about the company you do business with. AT&T has always respected the diversity that all people represent. In fact, AT&T has an environment in which gay, les . . . les . . . les . . . *lesbian* . . .

Well, the letter went on, but did you catch that? *They said it!* LESBIAN!! Yes, AT&T is reaching out and touching in a whole new way!! And why? Because everybody— including big corporations—thinks we have more money than straight America! I can see it now: we'll have them eating out of our hands, licking our boots! We'll start by taking over the travel industry! Hotels and motels will offer a *gay rate!* We'll be upgraded, and we'll be treated like the *queens* that we are!! (And when I say "queens," I'm including the les . . . les . . . *lesbians!!*)

andy
schell

Andy Schell initially produced *Confessions of a Boy Stewardess*—
which he also wrote and performs—on a shoestring budget, yet
he and the show received the kind of invaluable reviews that
any veteran showman would envy. Los Angeles critics, from the
mainstream and gay press as well as showbiz trade papers, blessed
the production with praise, including a promising forecast for
the career of the show's principal player.

"*Boy Stewardess* flies with humor," cheered the *Los Angeles
Times*. "Schell's imaginative flight [is] well worth taking."

"This is what we expect in Hollywood," wrote *Los Angeles
Theatres* magazine, "watching a star in the making, talented
before TV puts it in a small frame."

But Schell insists his motivation for mounting the show,
which debuted in 1994 at Theatre/Theater, was "not to do the
big Hollywood thing or make a big breakthrough." Rather, he

213

felt compelled to exercise his creativity. Otherwise, he states flatly, "I just couldn't pass out peanuts for another day."

You see, Schell is, indeed, a flight attendant for a no-frills airline. After a dozen years at his in-flight job, he says, "I did the show because my brain was about to atrophy and fall out!"

Actually, Schell's comedy career had gotten off the ground several years prior to *Boy Stewardess*. He was a member of the renowned improv group The Groundlings, which launched the careers of many comics, including *Saturday Night Live* alumna Julia Sweeney (known for her androgynous character Pat), whom Schell worked alongside.

A number of reviews agreed with the *L.A. Reader*, which noted, "[Schell] recalls the manic brilliance of Robin Williams." Rubber faced and lovably giddy onstage, Schell has heard the comparison before. But, he says, "I never tried to imitate his style. If anything, I imitated Joan Rivers's style."

Rivers, too, apparently recognized a likeness in their sensibilities. As a young joke writer, Schell wrote gags for the comedienne while he was attending Kansas University. (He's responsible for some of Rivers's juicy jibes at Nancy Reagan!)

After he started working for an airline, Schell continued to submit material to Rivers, who has been known to take shots at flirty female flight attendants. But, ironically, reports the "boy stewardess," "I tried and tried, but she never bought any of my stewardess jokes!"

from *confessions of a boy stewardess*

andy: *(Speaking to the audience)* When I first got hired as a flight attendant, I thought to myself, "Hot damn! This is going to be one big orgiastic, gay bacchanal!" Well, of course, I got hired by the one good ol' boy, bubba airline in the country whose male flight attendants are all *straight!*

Straight male flight attendant—I thought that was an oxymoron. Not at my airline. I'm the little token that slipped through the cracks. But at all other airlines they're gay. And gay guys *love* to be flight attendants. We are *so* into it. I was at this foofy pool party once up in the Hollywood Hills, and this group of guys migrated to one end of the pool and spent the whole afternoon talking about their flying jobs.

(He recreates the party, playing each character.)

steward #1: I've been working a lot of flights to Milan and Rome lately. Italy was teeming with testosterone—it's better than going to Home Depot.

steward #2: I'm based in Seattle, so I fly Far East. Asian men are so submissive they'll do *anything* for you—it's better than going to Neiman-Marcus.

steward #3: I prefer domestic trips. It is too complicated to learn how to speak Italian or Mandarin, when you simply want to say to someone, "Hey, I like your shoes!"

andy: (To the audience) I wanted to tell them that I flew for Desert Airlines, but I knew that they would look at me like I was the white trash of the industry, and say, "Desert Airlines? Isn't that the bargain airline where the flight attendants wear shorts, and they sing, and the plane stops three times between L.A. and Phoenix?"

I tried a different tack—something that was topical at the time—"Hey guys, how about those elections in South Africa?"

steward #3: I saw something on CNN about South Africa, and I just have to say, I love the clothes those people wear. The minute that report was over I flew to Johannesburg and bought a bright orange dashiki, which was really risky for me because I'm a winter, I'm not an autumn. But I'm telling you it's perfect for all occasions—I vacuum in it!

andy: (To the audience) OK, so we're a different kind of world traveler!

You just better hope that we're working your flight, because gay guys definitely make better flight attendants. Our uniforms are cleaned and pressed, our cuticles are cut, our makeup is blended—it doesn't stop right along the jaw line like the women's does.

And if you're in first class, that gay attendant will carve

you a flawless cut of roast. He'll pour your wine with the bottle six inches from the glass without spilling a drop. And for dessert, he'll top off your ice cream sundae by taking that can of whipped cream, turning it upside down, and with one press of that talented finger he'll recreate Michelangelo's *David*. Of course, David's penis is way out of scale, and sometimes it's so large it separates from his torso and falls onto your tray. Who says flying isn't fun anymore?!

Besides, the alternative is to be served by one of those *oxymoronic*, straight male flight attendants. Believe me, straight guys do *not* know how to make sculpture out of whipped cream. Their hair is greasy, their fingernails are dirty, and they spill the food and drinks. And I've never met one who wasn't a blatant puss hound. I've actually seen a straight male flight attendant sit down on an armrest in the middle of a flight and say to a woman . . .

(Andy plays both the man and the woman.)

straight male flight attendant: So . . . you come here often?

woman passenger: *(Crying)* No. I'm going to a funeral.

straight male flight attendant: A funeral . . . great . . . anyone I might know?

woman passenger: *(Crying harder)* My grandmother.

straight male flight attendant: So . . . you like funerals? 'Cause you look mighty fine in black.

(She runs up the aisle, to the lavatory.)

straight male flight attendant: *(Chuckles to himself)* She'll be back.

andy: *(To the audience)* Of course, straight male stewards are nothing compared to straight male *pilots.* The image Hollywood has created of the airline pilot is this tall, debonair guy with a golden tan acquired during his layover in Saint Croix. The guy with just a wisp of gray at each temple. His blue eyes deeper than the sky through which he navigates. His strong voice commanding the same degree of attention as that massive fuselage of a penis he uses to put a smile on the face of Third World stewardesses everywhere.

Ladies and gentlemen, that is the Hollywood version only. Most of these guys are ex–military pilots. Remember those guys in ROTC when you were in college? The goofy haircuts, the high-water pants, the shiny shoes? They dated their friends' sisters, they never did drugs, they had no rhythm? They jacked off to that Farrah Fawcett poster?

They're airline pilots now. My life is in their hands. Scary.

Thank God we have women pilots now. And, of course, some of them are our sisters. I introduced myself to one of our women captains once, putting out my hand to shake. She almost crushed it.

(Andy plays both the woman pilot and himself.)

carla, the pilot: *(With a tough voice, while shaking his hand)* Hi, I'm Carla.

andy: Ow! You're hurting me!

carla: Buck up, you little pair of panties. Now get me some coffee.

andy: *(Rubbing his damaged hand)* OK. How do you like it?

carla: Hot and black, just like my wom . . . I mean, just black.

andy: Yes, captain!

(To the audience again)

They may be gruff, but I'd rather fly with lesbian pilots any day. If they had to make an emergency landing, you just know those gals could land a 737 on a golf course!

scott
silverman

"I love cars *so* much!" gushes Scott Silverman, speaking like the true Southern Californian that he is. "Cars are *so* L.A.!" He loves everything automotive—except, perhaps, for car phones. "I think car phones are a little dangerous," he says. "My parents have one in their car, which is great, except when I'm speeding along at ninety miles an hour and the phone rings and scares me to death. Of course, it's my mom. 'Hi, hon, where are you?' 'Well, right now I'm in the *back* of a Buick LeSabre!' "

In 1991, Silverman hopped in his Acura Integra (which he translates as "Japanese for 'Honda Civic on an ego trip' ") and headed north. Reaching San Francisco, he recalls, "I got out of my car and I'm like, 'I'm home. This is where I belong!' I've never been able to shed that feeling."

One of his first stops was Open Mike Night at Josie's Cabaret & Juice Joint. What did the self-described car fanatic joke about his first time onstage? What else? "I talked about driving up there! I did a joke about passive-aggressive tailgating; they don't honk or beam their lights, they just reach in and change your stereo."

Silverman says he no longer refers to his Acura Integra on-stage. "They're not very funny," he says analytically. "Honda CRXs, though, I've found are a *scream* for some reason!"

Switching gears, Silverman explains what prompted him to do stand-up: "I was speaking in front of classes at Cal State, Northridge, as part of a gay and lesbian speakers bureau. Other people had these horror stories about being thrown out of the house because they're gay. Then I'd get up and I was like, 'Oh, my parents are more into this gay thing than I am,' and it would make people laugh."

The appeal of stand-up comedy in general, he says, "is getting to know a person's quirks and personality. I've got a real quirky life and personality, and it's not just because I like cars or stuff like that. Much of it is tied in to the fact that I'm gay.

"Most of what's really positive about me is my homosexuality, because that's my capacity to love. I think that's something everybody can relate to; everybody's looking for that special kind of love."

"honey, i thought this would interest you . . ."

My family is very supportive of the fact that I'm gay. They live in Southern California, and they came up to San Francisco to visit me and to go to the Gay Pride parade. They had a great time. In fact, my mother had a better time than I did. I think she's worried that if she doesn't keep reminding me that I'm gay, I'll forget and she'll get kicked out of P-FLAG—Parents and Friends of Lesbians and Gays.

My lifestyle must drive her crazy. Here I am frittering away my gayness, hanging out with miniskirted, makeup-wearing *übergirls*. I'm living for fast cars and rock and roll, and she has to drag me off to Gay Pride like it's the first day of kindergarten.

"Ma, I don't wanna go! There's all those gay people there and it's really *hot . . . !*"

She really gets into marching in the parade. She was working the crowd. I began to get jealous. I'm like, "Mom, you wouldn't be here if it wasn't for *me!*" She was working the crowd so hard! She was waving and carrying on, like, "*Love you! Love you!*" These guys along the way yelled out at her, "*Get it, girl!*" She asked me, "Honey, what does 'Get it, girl' mean?" I'm like, "Well, Mom, in this case it's sort of the gay stamp of approval." So she shouted back to them, "Well, you get it, too, girls!"

My stepfather marched with us, and they gave him a sign that said, MY SON IS GAY, AND THAT'S OK! He thought that was really boring, so he rewrote the sign to say, MY SON IS A QUEEN, AND THAT'S PEACHY-KEEN!

Next I hear my mom chanting, "We're here, we're queer, get used to it!" And I remind her, "Uh, Mom, you are not queer." And out of the corner of her mouth, she crabs at me, "Sssssssh, honey! Don't be disrespectful of your mother!"

After they returned home, my mother started sending me a Readers Digest–like personal-interest compilation of the Los Angeles Times. The articles—clipped like coupons and efficiently stapled together at the corners—fall out of the envelope in the correct order, with a cute little yellow Post-it note affixed, marked with her observations and little asides. Like, "Look, honey, it's our girl Madonna at an AIDS benefit in Beverly Hills." 'Cause you know I never would have noticed Madonna in the picture if Mom hadn't pointed it out to me!

Finally, I had to say, "Mom, enough with the gay articles. I know all I need to know about being gay. I'll take it from here and start doing some field research!"

Even my grandmother is cool about the fact that I'm gay. The only problem that she has is that I'm Jewish and I do not date Jewish guys. She's afraid it's going to have a negative effect on our children.

There was one person who wasn't really thrilled when I

came out to him—my real father. He was worried that I was going to be gay when I was eight years old because my mother put a plant in my room. He thought it would make me "funny." Which it did, when I smoked it.

My real father and I don't understand each other. He just got married for the third time; this time, to a woman who is six days older than I am. When we have arguments, he goes, "You know, Scott, I just don't understand your generation." And I'm like, "Well, gee, Dad, why did you marry into it?"

jeanne wiley

60 Minutes called Orange County, California, "a bastion of Republican conservatism." It's the birthplace of Richard M. Nixon, and it's the origin of nationally broadcast right-wing television programming. It's also the birthplace and still the home of Jeanne Wiley. The comic has taken her act on the road across the country, but, she maintains, she especially loves performing on her home turf. "Orange County *needs* entertainment—*wild* entertainment," she says.

At the Orange County Gay & Lesbian Pride Celebration on the campus of the University of California, Irvine, Wiley blasts onto the main stage wearing a black leather jacket, with a bushy tuft of green hair sprouting from her otherwise shaved head. (Hairstyle and color subject to frequent change.) In contrast, a tasteful plaid and pleated skirt completes her ensemble. "I went through twelve years of Catholic school," she explains. "I'm wearing plaids again; I'm working it out, I'm doing well." In her act, Wiley often speaks of her upbringing at an all–girls Catholic school. "I *have* to talk about it," she insists. "It saves me a lot of money on therapy."

In fact, there may not be a single facet of the comic's life which she *doesn't* share freely with her audiences. Says Wiley, "Professionally, I made the choice that I'm going to deal with touchy subjects: I talk about sex, I talk about bondage. The audience sees the leather look, which I *am* into, and they expect this bad girl. They expect me to be angry and mean. But then, all of a sudden, I'm likeable. They hear me talking about things they can all relate to, like Etch-A-Sketch and Slinky." (Onstage, she reminisces, "Remember Slinky? *Minutes* of fun! Unfortunately, I grew up living in a one-story house!")

Indeed, to some, she may be perceived as a paradox personified: Jeanne Wiley is the all-American *leather* girl next door. "Orange County is all suburban neighborhoods, and when you live next door to somebody who's gay and out, like myself, they see that we have a flower bed, we go grocery shopping. They see I have a smile on my face and my lover's hand in mine," she says. "That's why I advocate being out—so that people know that, yeah, we're happy."

onstage

no time off for good behavior

I'm a second-generation Southern Californian. Specifically, Orange County. I know that Orange County has a reputation for being conservative and stuffy, but both my parents were actually the type that the rest of the world thinks of when they think of Californians. Yes, they were surfers! Surfer parents! As an adult, I've had to join a self-help group. Perhaps you've heard of it: ACAC, Adult Children of a Californian.

Thanks to this group I was able to tap into painful memories of my father, all blurry-eyed as he towered over my tiny, sleeping form and said things like, "Wake up, Dudette. The waves don't wait for anyone. Let's go for it!" Or the oft-repeated "When I was your age, I was expected to get a dozen good waves in before school; I expect no less of you!"

ACAC helped me in other ways too. I became strong enough to come out to my parents—as a nonsurfer.

What an ordeal that was! Such a vivid memory. I walked out to the yard where they were sex-waxing their boards, and I said, "Chickster . . . Kahuna . . ."—that's Mom and Dad—"I have something to tell you. I'm not like the other kids. I have different interests, different friends . . ." Finally, I just blurted it out. "I'm moving *in-land! I want to read!*"

My father reacted first. "Whoa, Dudette, that totally bites!"

My mother took it a little better. "You know, that does blow . . . but can I have your wet suit?"

I attended Catholic school for twelve years, with no time off for good behavior. It was an Irish Catholic school,

Saint Columban. He was Ireland's patron saint of car bombs. The nuns that educated me came directly off the potato boat. You have to understand, these people grew up in a war zone, which existed ever since the Protestants and the Catholics first learned they could throw rocks at each other! Apparently, battle fatigue would set in, and for R&R, they'd ship these little ninja nuns—these commandoes for Christ, if you will—off to Orange County, California, to teach small children.

With the compassion and patience of a marine drill sergeant, they turned corporal punishment into an art form. Here I was at a young, impressionable age, on a weekly basis being dragged by my ear down a long corridor by this woman dressed in a black robe that flowed to the ground, screaming religious taunts at me in a thick Irish brogue. She'd throw me into a dingy janitor's closet, bend me over and beat my schoolgirl butt with this cheeseboard-looking paddle that had holes in it to raise welts. All because I "brazenly" chewed gum in class! I think about it now and I think, "My God! That kind of kinky stuff would cost me big bucks today!" I know—I checked. And the nun's costume is extra. (Oops, I share too much.)

I'm now happily married. I know, it's not "legal" yet. But, hell, I have to take out the trash, share the remote, call home if I'm going to be late, share a sock drawer . . . I *am* married!

We had a ceremony that consisted of traditional wedding customs, and we also expressed ourselves by adding our own personal touches. For example:

We exchanged rings (traditional). Then we pierced our navels with them—our personal touch!

We took two candles, which represented our lives apart, and with them ignited a single candle to signify our lives joined together (traditional). Then we dripped hot wax on our bare skin—yup, our personal touch!

We wore dresses (traditional). They were black patent leather—*that's us!*

My wife and I received many interesting wedding gifts. My favorite was a gift certificate to an adult store. If you haven't been to a naughty store recently, then you must go immediately. The new products are quite innovative. Remember Hoppity Hop, the kids' toy that was a large rubber ball with a handle that you rode? Well, they have a new and improved adult version of something like that. They've now affixed a large phallus to this thing! Talk about fun! A little hard to explain those noises to the neighbors, but . . . ! (Oops. Am I sharing too much again?)

When my wife and I moved in together, I moved from a house that I shared with four other women. If you've ever had roommates, you know how hard it is to get along with someone you're not sleeping with!

One of my roommates had a vibrator that plugged directly into the wall socket. Have you ever been watching TV, and someone vacuums or uses the blender? You know how the TV gets all those lines across it? Well, the same thing would happen when this roommate kicked her vibrator on. No matter what we were watching, it suddenly turned into an episode of *Outer Limits*. A deep, serious voice would come on, "Do not attempt to adjust your television set; your roommate is masturbating. When she gets off, we will resume normal television transmission."

That was the thing—it wasn't so bad that we knew she was masturbating, but we also knew precisely when she was done! The lines on the TV would go away—the whole house would heave a big sigh, even the cats!

* * *

I talk about sex very frankly onstage, and after my shows, I've often been asked for sexual advice or tips from young, fledgling lesbians ("leslings," I call them). In particular, I was recently asked for pointers regarding oral sex with women. I'll share it with you.

You must be creative to be a great lover. Try tracing the alphabet with your tongue. By the time you get to the lower case *m*, things will be happening! Just don't make the mistake I did and tell your partner what you're doing. You'll get help from the sidelines—"Dot the *i*, dot the *i* right now! OK, now *l*, *m*—capital, lowercase, capital, lowercase—*n*, *o* . . . quick, go to *z*! Yes, yes, that's it!"

When I give this advice, gay men don't get it. They're like, "We just do *o*!"

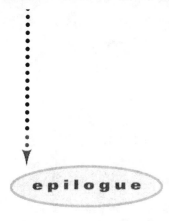

meryl cohn, aka ms. behavior

predictions for gay and lesbian comics (and the audiences who love them)

What does the future hold for openly gay and lesbian comics?

I posed this question to someone who routinely answers probing questions from folks in the gay and lesbian community —Meryl Cohn, aka Ms. Behavior, columnist and author of *Do What I Say: Ms. Behavior's Guide to Gay & Lesbian Etiquette.* While offering good-sense advice, this out and proud lesbian's tongue is always—where else?—planted firmly in her cheek.

Her qualifications for dishing out counsel? "I had been a psychology major at Smith College," explains Cohn, "and one of the things I realized was that I lacked the patience to listen to people for fifty minutes at a time, but I still had this impulse to tell people what to do."

Before Cohn gave birth to her opinionated alter ego in 1991, she worked as a journalist writing reviews, interviews, and even a health column for *Bay Windows,* Boston's gay weekly newspaper. All the while, her humorous bent was brewing, until it finally burst out in the form of Ms. Behavior's advice and etiquette column.

"There's a certain humor and campiness that has begun to cross the lines in the community from men to women, and I think that's a good thing," observes Cohn. "It's partly happened through entertainment—through singers and comics—and partly through ways that the community has begun to interact a little bit more."

Since the release of her book, Ms. Behavior's column has been syndicated in gay and lesbian publications nationwide, and she's received limitless correspondence seeking her opinion. Add to that one more . . .

＊　＊　＊

Dear Ms. Behavior,

Over the last couple of years, I've been talking with performers who are openly gay and lesbian. As unbelievable as it would have seemed even ten years ago, there are now enough out and proud stand-up comics to honor in a book.

Ms. Behavior, what impact do you think this phenomenon will have on the entertainment industry? Do you think straight audiences would accept it if 10 percent of the TV characters were queer (as in the real world)? And what about young gay and lesbian people with showbiz aspirations? To be out or not to be out, that is the query (to rephrase William Shakespeare—a bi, by the way).

Best wishes to you and all who are living and laughing out,

Ed Karvoski Jr.

Dear Ed and gay and lesbian friends and straight thrill seekers:

Like most of her gay and lesbian brothers and sisters, Ms. Behavior is thrilled to see that queer humor is no longer relegated to the arena of belittling jokes and funny subtext. In thinking about how far we've come in being "everywhere," it's easy to forget that vaudeville, World War II camp shows, and the earliest form of television thrived on cross-dressing. Lots of us are too young to remember Milton Berle's dress, but we've all heard about it. And that ugly frock was at least a primitive form of genderfuck, which has long been an area of amusement to straight audiences, as well as gay men and lesbians.

Although Ms. Behavior is committed to her position as an advice and etiquette columnist, her people-pleasing streak pushes her to rise to the invitation to be psychic, both predicting and fantasizing about the delightful future for gay and lesbian comedy . . .

Imagine straight female comics donning leather jackets at home, facing the mirror, and practicing mouthing the word "dildo." Envision babes from the suburbs endowed with large hairdos passing as femme lezbos like the fabulous Suzanne Westenhoefer (which means that they won't have to get tattoos or other accoutrements for authenticity, like they would if they tried to emulate Lea DeLaria).

Straight male comics might stop imitating Seinfeld and instead try to incorporate a witty gay sensibility into their acts. Attempting to get in touch with their softer selves might mean cultivating interests in design, in musical divas from the seventies, and in toning their buttocks. The ironic side effect of this charade of homosexuality is that it will naturally make them more appealing to women. For a few of these folks, the true gift will be the revelation that they actually *are* gay, and their future routines will be about their own previous lack of enlightenment.

Hyperhet entertainer David Letterman might invite Keanu Reeves to table-dance on the desk and bare his chest, and Oprah might reveal that she's had fantasies about women. Gay and lesbian celebrity talk shows will pop up on all the networks. (Imagine Chastity Bono hosting a variety showcase for her Sapphically inclined friends. She will sing "I Got You, Babe" to her girlfriend, occasionally glancing toward her mother, sitting in the audience with tears smearing her makeup.)

Once people get used to funny queers onstage and on talk shows, sitcoms will be a natural extension. Interactive media will be a big boon to the queerification of sitcoms. Audiences will have choices about whether to watch regular reruns of popular shows or revised-format programming where the main character becomes gay. At the press of a button, Felix Unger is released from his sentence of bachelorhood and allowed to cruise in the park. Big butch Maude tells wormy Arthur she's leaving him for her gal pal. Rhoda Morgenstern confesses to Mary Richards that she wants to get in her pants (or, more precisely, her hip-hugger, bell-bottom, paisley-print pants), and they will have a one- or two-episode fling. And instead of taking off his shoes and donning a sweater and sneakers, Mr. Rogers is finally free to wear a colorful little shift and a pair of mules.

After an early flurry of right-wing protest, more hetero viewers will readily adapt to the queering of entertainment. Straights will first write letters to *TV Guide* complaining about having to watch homosexuals call each other "honey." They'll initially boycott products sponsored by advertisers on gay-themed shows, but their plan will backfire when sponsors realize how huge a market 10 percent really is. Once that happens, advertisers will court the gay and lesbian audience that has been waiting all these years to be addressed. Imagine Melissa Etheridge as spokesperson for the Tofu Council of America, creating such a demand for this spongy product that she creates a soybean shortage. Soon the gay advertising wave takes over, with Elton John for Foster Grant sunglasses, RuPaul for Big and Tall stores, Bob Paris for Thigh Masters, Martina Navratilova for Snap-On Tools . . .

Initially, there may be some segregated gay and lesbian shows (the equivalent of early black entertainment, like *Sanford and Son*), followed by the integration of lesbian and gay characters in starring roles in "regular" shows. There will be room for gay protagonists, instead of just "the dyke/fag next door" parts. The overall cultural effect on straight society will be that instead of just taking on homo style and homo design, hets can also absorb some homo humor, which will undoubtedly be an improvement.

But with all of this, can we ever expect 10 percent of the characters on TV to be queer characters, reflecting numbers consistent with real life? Ms. Behavior prays for that day and lights lots of patchouli-scented candles, but she's not holding her breath. Or at least it won't happen until more people, including performers, *come out*.

Yes, Ms. Behavior does like to imagine what might happen if every gay or lesbian actor, writer, director, and producer came crashing out of the closet. Hollywood would be turned upside down and inside *out*. No longer would there be a fear of careers being destroyed if a Hollywood hunk was seen holding hands with another superstar stud. Leading women would clamor to confess their lesbianism, which would suddenly be cool.

The initial backlash from the right, which would scurry to take hold of both television programming and film-making, might be painfully macho: more war movies and cowboy movies would be made. Perhaps you couldn't turn on your TV without being assaulted by reruns of *Bonanza* mixed with gross superhetero flicks like *Porky's, Porky's II,* and *Porky's Revenge. Rambo* Month would become a frequent occurrence.

But as the gay sensibility trickled into straight society, sitcoms with believable gay characters might emerge. Maybe quirky traits and interests would be allowed to be expressed, and characters would actually be able to do the nasty (what a relief!). Gay and lesbian orientation would be neither the focus—like it is in those "Oh my God, my son is a homosexual" made-for-TV dramas—or totally ignored, as it is in sitcoms which go over the top in trying to make their queer characters "just like everyone else."

Ms. Behavior is hoping for the emergence of a climate in which it is natural for gay and lesbian comics to be out. But, of course, it is only coming out to begin with that allows for overall acceptance. Being funny is about being able to tap into your biggest, truest, most whole self. The more authentically and openly yourself you are, the more there is for the audience to relate to. Plus, when you reveal who you are, you have much more potential to be hilariously funny. (If you have trouble envisioning that, think about how much more amusing it would be if Lucy from *Peanuts*—a real dyke if Ms. Behavior ever saw one—was allowed to pursue Peppermint Patty, instead of fey little

Schroeder!) So, since you asked, Ms. Behavior's advice to young new performers is . . . swing out sisters and brothers, and be the biggest, baddest, gayest self you can be!

In Love and Light,
Ms. Behavior

final

words

The work of openly gay and lesbian comics—and all gay and lesbian artists—is what is really going to make a difference for our people. The activists are there to fend off the attacks and to protect our backs, but the artists can change minds faster. Historically, that's been true: it's the arts that change society. The creative process happens before the rhetoric.

Gay and lesbian comics are certainly on the front lines —way out there. Some people see these comics as an entertainment value; I see it as a victory value.

—Ivy Bottini, maverick activist for the
gay/lesbian and women's movements

acknowledgments

I would like to express my gratitude to the many people who helped make *A Funny Time to Be Gay* possible. First and foremost, much gratitude goes to my literary agent Alison Picard and editor Cindy Gitter, both for saying yes and for offering helpful guidance.

Many thanks to the magazine and newspaper editors who accepted my articles about gay and lesbian comics before the topic received mainstream media attention. My appreciation particularly goes to French Wall at *The Guide*, David Kalmansohn and Monica Trasandes at *Frontiers*, David Hodgson at *California Nightlife*, and Rudy Kikel at *Bay Windows*.

And, of course, a great big thank-you to *all* openly gay and lesbian comics for making it A FUNNY TIME TO BE GAY.

Special appreciation goes to the following humorists for sharing their witty words:

Robin Tyler: *Still a Bridesmaid, Never a Groom.* Copyright © 1997 by Robin Tyler. Printed by permission of the author.

Tom Ammiano: *A Queen in Search of a Motif.* Copyright © 1997 by Tom Ammiano. Printed by permission of the author.

Suzy Berger: *Once upon a Time. . .* Copyright © 1997 by Suzy Berger. Printed by permission of the author.

Monica Palacios: An adapted excerpt from *Latin Lezbo Comic.* Copyright © 1995 Monica Palacios. Reprinted from *Latinas on Stage: Practice and Theory,* edited by Alicia Arrizón and Lillian Manzor by permission of the author, editors, and Third Woman Press, Berkeley, California.

Karen Ripley: *I'm Just a Channel.* Copyright © 1997 by Karen Ripley. Printed by permission of the author.

Romanovsky & Phillips: *The Homosexual Agenda and Functional Illiteracy.* Copyright © 1995 by Romanovsky & Phillips; "If There Is a God" copyright © 1992 by Romanovsky; and "What Kind of Self-Respecting Faggot/Politically Correct Lesbian Am I?" copyright © 1994 by Romanovsky & Phillips. Reprinted by permission of the authors.

Danny Williams: *Common Ground.* Copyright © 1997 by Danny Williams. Printed by permission of the author.

Kate Clinton: *Holy Apologies* first appeared in *The Progressive* (Sept. 1995). Copyright © 1995 by Kate Clinton. Reprinted by permission of the author and *The Progressive,* 409 East Main Street, Madison, WI 53703.

Lynn Lavner: *Butch Fatale* and "A Lesbian Too Long." Copyright © 1992 by Lynn Lavner. Printed by permission of the author.

Danny McWilliams: *Under My Spell.* Copyright © 1997 by Danny McWilliams. Printed by permission of the author.

Judy Carter: *Nice Girls Don't Say Things Like That.* Copyright © 1997 by Judy Carter. Printed by permission of the author.

Michael Dane: *Views from the Fence.* Copyright © 1997 by Michael Dane. Printed by permission of the author.

Steve Moore: *You Folks Are Killing Me!* Copyright © 1997 by Steve Moore. Printed by permission of the author.

Barry Steiger: *Aluminum!* Copyright © 1997 by Barry Steiger. Printed by permission of the author.

Jason Stuart: *My Boyfriend's Black (and I'm Gonna Be in Trouble).* Copyright © 1997 by Jason Stuart. Printed by permission of the author.

Bob Smith: *Out Tonight* (from Bob Smith's apearance on *The Tonight*

photo credits

Robin Tyler
Photo courtesy Robin Tyler

Tom Ammiano
Photo courtesy Tom Ammiano
Photo © Rink/Foto SF

Suzy Berger
Photo courtesy Suzy Berger
Photo by Micque Li

Monica Palacios
Photo courtesy Monica Palacios
Photo by Becky Villasenor

Karen Ripley
Photo courtesy Karen Ripley
Photo by Micque Li

Romanovsky & Phillips
Photo courtesy Romanovsky &
Phillips
Photo by Irene Young

Danny Williams
Photo courtesy Danny Williams
Photo by RAM Studios

Kate Clinton
Photo courtesy Kate Clinton
Photo by Joe Henson

Jaffe Cohen
Photo courtesy Jaffe Cohen

Lynn Lavner
Photo courtesy Lynn Lavner
Photo by Anita Shevett

Danny McWilliams
Photo courtesy Danny McWilliams
Photo by Michael Wakefield

Judy Carter
Photo courtesy Judy Carter
Photo by John Mejia

Michael Dane
Photo courtesy Michael Dane

Steve Moore
Photo courtesy Steve Moore
Photo by Attila Aszodi

Barry Steiger
Photo courtesy Barry Steiger
Photo by Marvin Rinning

Jason Stuart
Photo courtesy Jason Stuart
Photo by Kevin Merrill

Bob Smith
Photo courtesy Bob Smith and
HBO

Suzanne Westenhoefer
Photo courtesy Suzanne
Westenhoefer
Photo by Glenn Jussen

Matina Bevis
Photo courtesy Matina Bevis
Photo by Lee Issacc

Joan Jett Blakk
Photo courtesy Joan Jett Blakk

Mark Davis
Photo courtesy Mark Davis
Photo by Franco, RAM Studios

Monica Grant
Photo courtesy Monica Grant
Photo by Julie Riffle

Robin Greenspan
Photo courtesy Robin Greenspan
Photo by Tom Lascher

E. L. Greggory
Photo courtesy E. L. Greggory

Paul Jacek
Photo courtesy Paul Jacek
Photo by Paul Greggory

Sabrina Matthews
Photo courtesy Sabrina Matthews
Photo by Bonnie Daley

Lynda Montgomery
Photo courtesy Lynda Montgomery

Marilyn Pittman
Photo courtesy Marilyn Pittman
Photo © Debra St. John

Andy Schell
Photo courtesy Andy Schell
Photo by Mel Cavalier

Scott Silverman
Photo courtesy Scott Silverman
Photo by Kim Loeffler

Jeanne Wiley
Photo courtesy Jeanne Wiley
Photo by Judith P. Loniak

Meryl Cohn
Photo courtesy Meryl Cohn
Photo by Benno Friedman

comics listing

Following is a list of comics who have provided contact information for the purpose of bookings and public relations. Every effort has been made to ensure the accuracy of the listings that appear in this book. However, changes in representation and contact information, as well as typographical errors, are possible. Neither the author nor the publisher is responsible for misdirected correspondence or returned mail.

Tom Ammiano
401 Van Ness Avenue
San Francisco, CA 94102
(415) 554-5144

ANT
Representation
The Agency
1800 Avenue of the Stars
Suite 400
Los Angeles, CA 90068
(310) 551-3000

Michele Balan
(212) 592-3902
Representation
Joan Martin
(619) 322-5778

Jackie Beat
1845 North Gramercy Place
Suite 306
Los Angeles, CA 90028
(213) 465-6325

Suzy Berger
Representation
Andy Valvur
Jennifer Spalding and Associates
1592 Union Street
Suite 93
San Francisco, CA 94123
(415) 386-5996

Matina Bevis
Representation
Best Girl Productions
1706 N.E. 7th Avenue
Ft. Lauderdale, FL 33305
(954) 768-9742

Joan Jett Blakk
281 Clinton Park
San Francisco, CA 90103
(415) 553-4164

Amy Boyd
3970 Barner Avenue
Oakland, CA 94602
phone/fax: (510) 482-6280

Maureen Brownsey
Representation
Odd Girl Out Productions
phone/fax: (415) 550-1660

Bruno
1400 North Gardner Street
Suite 3
Los Angeles, CA 90046
(213) 878-0255

Scott Capurro
(415) 885-6661
Representation
Vivienne Clone
The Richard Stone Partnership
25 Whitehall
London
SWIA 2BS
0171-839-6421

Karla Carmony
1600 Beverly Place
Berkeley, CA 94707
(510) 528-8397

Shann Carr
P.O. Box 31860
San Francisco, CA 94131
(510) 937-HAHA

Judy Carter
2112 Walnut Avenue
Venice, CA 90291
(800) 4-COMICS
fax: (310) 398-8046

Maggie Cassella
Representation
Leslie Wimmer
White Porch Booking
9 Highland Avenue
Haverhill, MA 01830
phone/fax: (508) 372-4665

Tory Christopher
P.O. Box 8424
Universal City, CA 91618
phone/fax: (213) 851-5627
e-mail: tc90046@aol.com
Representation
Janice Stanley
The William Carroll Agency
(818) 848-9948

Kate Clinton
Representation
Steve Levine
ICM
8942 Wilshire Boulevard
Los Angeles, CA 90211
phone/fax: (310) 550-4000

Jaffe Cohen
343 West 12 Street
Suite 5A
New York, NY 10014
(212) 627-7988

**Meryl Cohn,
aka Ms. Behavior**
Representation
Gloria Loomis
133 East 35 Street
Suite 1
New York, NY 10016
(212) 532-0080
e-mail: msbehavior@aol.com

Cowboy Girl, aka Lisa Lerner
P.O. Box 2001
New York, NY 10009
(212) 228-4462

Sara Cytron
Representation
Harriet Malinowitz
23 Waverly Place
Suite 6H
New York, NY 10003
(212) 995-5526

Michael Dane
8 Park Plaza
Suite 218
Boston, MA 02116
(800) 935-4944

Mark Davis
2711½ Silver Ridge Avenue
Los Angeles, CA 90039
(213) 664-6939

Frank DeCaro
Representation
Angela Miller
The Miller Agency
801 West End Avenue
New York, NY 10025
(212) 866-6110
fax: (212) 866-0068

**Kevin DiLallo and Jack
Krumholtz
(authors of *The Unofficial
Gay Manual*)**
Representation
Sloan Harris
ICM
40 West 57 Street
New York, NY 10019
(212) 556-5721
fax: (212) 556-5665

**Dos Fallopia
(Lisa Koch and Peggy Platt)**
Representation
Tongueinchic Productions
1202 East Pike.
Suite 712
Seattle, WA 98122
phone/fax: (206) 760-8864
e-mail: Tunginchic@aol.com

Lynda Finn
P.O. Box 3112
Madison, WI 53704

The Five Lesbian Brothers
(Theater Company)
Representation
Sama Blackwell
225 East 25 Street
Suite 3D
New York, NY 10010
(212) 481-4168
e-mail: Sam710@aol.com

Emmett Foster
312 West 51 Street
Suite 3R
New York, NY 10019
(212) 265-1714

4 Big Girls
343¹/₂ 17 Avenue
Seattle, WA 98122
(206) 323-5171

Mimi-Freed
Representation
Marcus Maguire
Sphere Entertainment
1752 Thornwood Drive
Concord, CA 94521
(510) 682-4141

**The Gay Comedy Jam:
Freedom Tour
(Scott Kennedy and
Kevin Maye)**
Representation
LoneStar Entertainment
5090 Richmond Avenue
Suite 168
Houston, TX 77056
phone/fax: (713) 840-1166

Marga Gomez
Representation
Irene Pinn, Management &
Development Company
1628 Marlay Drive
Los Angeles, CA 90069
(213) 650-2391
fax: (213) 650-3834

Monica Grant
Representation
Leslie Wimmer
White Porch Booking
9 Highland Avenue
Haverhill, MA 01830
phone/fax: (508) 372-4665

Robin Greenspan
(818) 816-6815

Michael Greer
Representation
Kinney Productions
The Hollywood Ardmore
1850 North Whitley
Suite 714
Hollywood, CA 90028
(213) 464-1065

E. L. Greggory
(213) 255-3203
fax: (213) 255-3205

James "Gypsy" Haake
Representation
Elinor Berger
The Irv Schechter Company
9300 Wilshire Boulevard
Beverly Hills, CA 90212
(310) 278-8070

Lacie Harmon
Representation
Marlyn Management
4378 Lankershim Boulevard
Universal City, CA 91602
(213) 483-2987
fax: (213) 483-1265

Paul Jacek
Representation
Clifford Bell
c/o "Tory Christopher's
Unchained Comedy"
P.O. Box 8424
Universal City, CA 91618
(213) 782-4030
fax: (213) 851-5627

Susan Jeremy
(212) 726-1851 or
(212) 505-1763

Ed Karvoski Jr.
7985 Santa Monica Boulevard
Suite 109-488
West Hollywood, CA 90046

Keegan & Lloyd
(Tom Keegan and
Davidson Lloyd)
2118 Wilshire Boulevard
Suite 288
Santa Monica, CA 90403
(310) 452-6314

Lisa Kron
Representation
International Production
Associates
584 Broadway
Suite 1008
New York, NY 10009
(212) 925-2100
fax: (212) 925-2426

Elvira Kurt
phone/fax: (416) 488-6575
Representation
Jeff Andrews Talent House
186 Dupont Street
Toronto, Ontario M5R-2E6
Canada
(416) 960-9686
fax: (416) 960-2314

Ladies on the Couch
(Kari Finn and Susan Howard)
2021 West Dickens
Chicago, IL 60647
(312) 772-7580

Lynn Lavner
Representation
Ardis Sperber
Bent Productions
480 East 17 Street
Brooklyn, NY 11226
(718) 284-4473
fax: (718) 282-8358

Shelly Mars
Representation
Carrellas & Cooper
309 West 57 Street
Suite 803
New York, NY 10019
(212) 265-3796
fax: (212) 581-0299

Sabrina Matthews
Representation
Jackman & Taussig
Entertainment
1815 Butler Avenue
Suite 120
Los Angeles, CA 90025
(310) 478-6641
fax: (310) 444-8935

**Steven J. McCarthy,
aka Madame Dish**
Madame Dish Productions
P.O. Box 9164
North Hollywood, CA 91609
hot line: (818) 759-1770
phone/fax: (818) 760-0594
Representation
Steve Stevens
(213) 850-5761

John McGivern
Representation
Katharine Reilly
The Reilly Company
2579 Fire Mountain Drive
Oceanside, CA 92054
(619) 433-0333
fax: (619) 433-0505

Danny McWilliams
(212) 866-8577

Lynda Montgomery
1351 Park Avenue
Long Beach, CA 90804
(310) 597-5905

Steve Moore
(818) 763-8772

Naked Brunch
(Improv Group)
Naked Brunch Productions
P.O. Box 91
Boston, MA 02123
(617) 450-9485

Rob Nash
(713) 465-5500
Representation
Stars, The Agency
777 Davis Street
San Francisco, CA 94111
(415) 421-6272

The Nellie Olesons
(Queer Comedy Troupe)
Representation
Nora Burns
17 Cleveland Place
New York, NY 10012
(212) 941-8975

Over Our Heads
(Improv Group)
Representation
Karen Ripley
2550 Shattuck Avenue
Box 59
Berkeley, CA 94704
(510) 620-0970
e-mail: UmorMe@aol.com

Monica Palacios
2118 Wilshire Boulevard
Suite 374
Santa Monica, CA 90403
(310) 827-4793

Deb Parks-Satterfield
343$^{1}/_{2}$ 17 Avenue
Seattle, WA 98122
(206) 323-5171

Stephen Patterson
Representation
Ditto Productions
371 Fort Washington Avenue
Suite 5E
New York, NY 10033
phone/fax: (212) 923-9300

Janice Perry, aka Gal
Bedbug Inn
Ferrisburgh, VT 05456
(802) 877-3223

Marilyn Pittman
2261 Market Street
Suite 456
San Francisco, CA 94114
(415) 461-9410

Georgia Ragsdale
(213) 856-5664
Representation
Bill Melamed
The Producers Entertainment
Group, Inc.
9150 Wilshire Boulevard
Suite 205
Beverly Hills, CA 90212
(310) 285-0400

D.D. Rainbow
Representation
Rainbow Entertainment
6440 Bellingham Avenue
Suite 158
North Hollywood, CA 91606
(818) 569-5626

Karen S. Ripley
Representation
Shannon Bloom
2550 Shattuck Avenue
Box 59
Berkeley, CA 94704
(415) 661-3757 or
(510) 620-0970
fax: (415) 661-9058

Greg Roman
200 Clarendon Street
39th Floor
Boston, MA 02116
(617) 859-4097
fax: (617) 859-4077

Romanovsky & Phillips
Representation
Fresh Fruit Records
369 Montezuma Avenue
Suite 209
Santa Fe, NM 87501
(505) 989-8647
fax: (505) 989-7381

Andy Schell
Representation
Ty Harman
630 North Fairview Street
Burbank, CA 91505
(818) 842-6759

Scott Silverman
Representation
Patrick Baca
Artist Management West
103 North Clark Drive
Los Angeles, CA 90048
(310) 550-0028
fax: (310) 550-7730

Guy Silvestro
c/o Naked Brunch Productions
P.O. Box 91
Boston, MA 02123
(617) 450-9485
e-mail: cimocboy@aol.com

Bob Smith
Representation
Bob Read
Albrecht-Read Management
737 North Seward
Suite 1
Los Angeles, CA 90038
(213) 461-3200
fax: (213) 461-3468

**Split Britches Theater Company
(Peggy Shaw and Lois Weaver)**
75 East 4 Street
Suite 18
New York, NY 10003
(212) 473-6377

Barry Steiger
Representation
Craig Agency
8485 Melrose Place
Los Angeles, CA 90069
(213) 655-0236
fax: (213) 655-1491

Jason Stuart
758 North Hudson Avenue
Suite 5
Los Angeles, CA 90038
(213) 463-7026
fax: (213) 871-1808
Representation
Alroy/Schwartz
(818) 783-9575

Carmelita Tropicana
(212) 979-9225

Robin Tyler
Robin Tyler Productions, Inc.
15842 Chase Street
North Hills, CA 91343
(818) 893-4075
fax: (818) 893-1593

Suzanne Westenhoefer
Representation
Judy Dlugacz, A Management & Development Company
4400 Market Street
Oakland, CA 94608
(510) 655-0364
fax: (510) 655-4334

Jeanne Wiley
P.O. Box 862
Fullerton, CA 92632
(714) 578-0387

Danny Williams
401 Dolores
Suite 101
San Francisco, CA 94110
(415) 431-0777
fax: (415) 621-3248 (attention: Carl Wolf)

Karen Williams
Representation
Cheryl Reed
Bulleone Inc.
P.O. Box 32147
Euclid, OH 44132
voice mail: (800) 323-6036
(216) 289-2939
fax: (216) 289-5885

about the author

Ed Karvoski Jr. has worked as a comedy writer, a stand-up comedian, an actor, and a journalist. But he simply calls himself a Renaissance Queen.

As a comedy writer, Karvoski has written for Jay Leno, and radio deejays at CBS, NBC, and the BBC.

As a journalist, his entertainment reports have appeared in national magazines such as *The Advocate, Out, Poz,* and *The Guide.* He has also written for numerous regional publications, including *Frontiers, Bay Windows, Windy City Times, Dallas Voice, Front Page, Southern Voice, California Nightlife, Orange County Blade,* and *Gay People's Chronicle.*

As a performer, his television appearances include *Facts of Life, Fantasy Island,* and *As the World Turns.*

Self-described as "bicoastal, but all gay," Karvoski has lived in Boston, New York, and Los Angeles.